Rave Reviews

I remember getting a smallpox vaccine. It left a scar on my upper left arm that still looks like a little white circle. I also remember eating a little sugar cube that had something red on it, and that was my polio vaccine. My parents were very excited about the polio sugar cube. No one explained to me about the horrors of smallpox and polio or why I was getting a vaccination. Carole Marsh tells the fascinating history of these deadly illnesses and plenty more in *Outbreaks, Epidemics, & Pandemics*. The text is rich in historically accurate facts, timelines and vocabulary about some of the major diseases that have punctuated mankind's reign on earth as well as the anatomy of disease in general. Carole's signature storytelling style will have middle-schoolers taking this book to bed with them to read ahead. I had a career teaching middle school science and have always been fascinated by the microscopic world. I would have been thrilled to use *Outbreaks, Epidemics, & Pandemics* in my curriculum. This book is a fantastic educational resource that will no doubt inspire many future medical professionals, epidemiologists and microbiologists as they navigate their career paths.

—*Caroline Carpenter, retired science teacher*

I wish I could go back to middle school. We never had all-encompassing lessons that are integrated like Carole Marsh's Curriculum Lab. Our lessons were flat, boring, and rote. These are exciting, interesting and leave me wanting to know more about outbreaks, epidemics, and pandemics. Hats off to a super educator!

—*Nancy Waterhouse, New York/New Jersey*

Outbreaks, Epidemics, & Pandemics is full of facts and history that are not only honest and informative but also interesting and engaging. Pandemics and germs are an exciting subject, and this curriculum shows that! It teaches the history of germs and past outbreaks through stories and memorable facts that students will want to share and continue learning about.

—*Christina Yother Williams, designer*

The perfect blend of fact and fun to make learning about disease epidemics captivating for middle-schoolers. It's just the right amount of wit, information, and grossness to keep anyone coming back for more (wearing a face mask, of course!).

—*C.J. Ellison, author*

OUTBREAKS, EPIDEMICS, & PANDEMICS

Including the Worldwide COVID-19 Pandemic

CAROLE MARSH

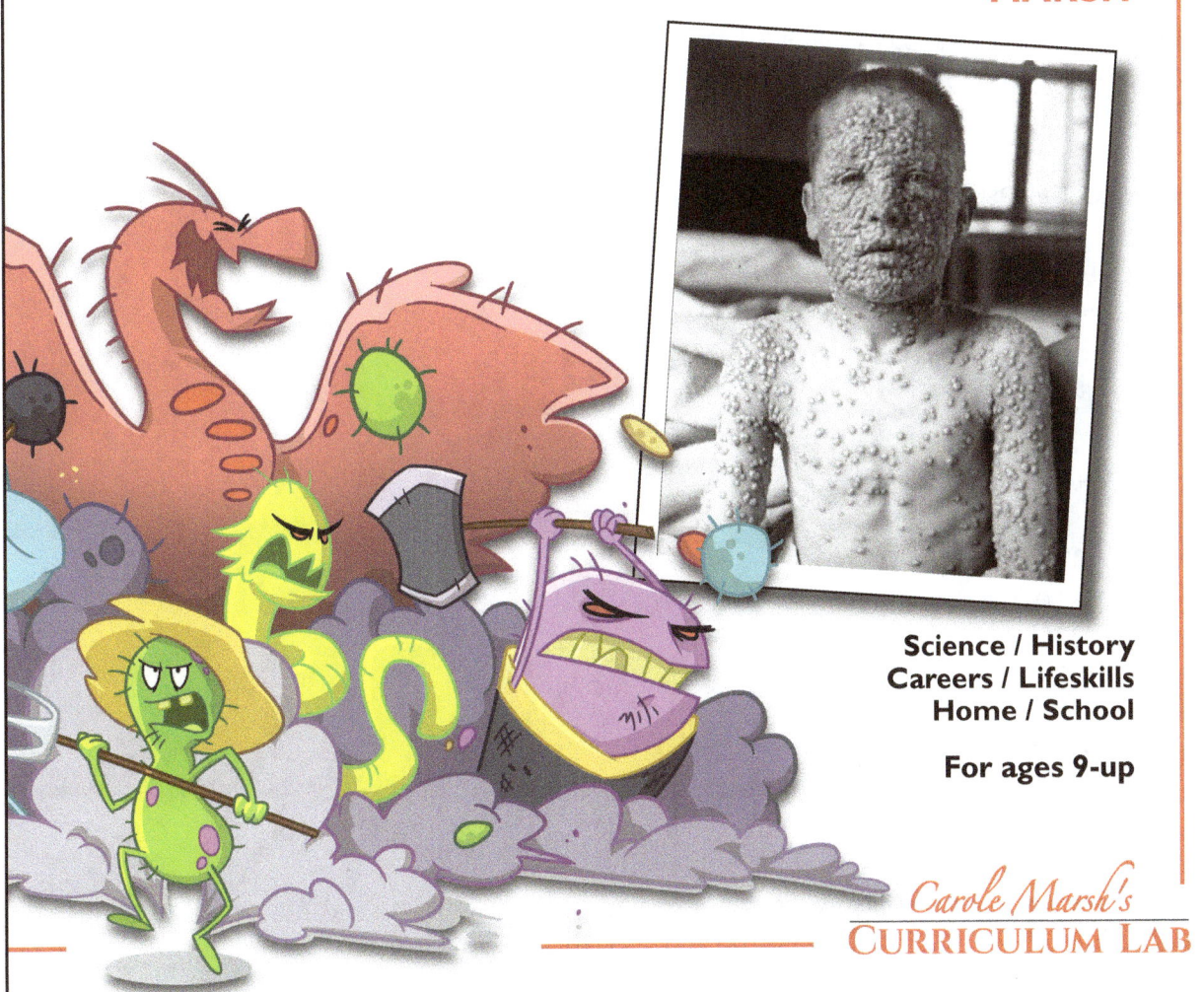

Science / History
Careers / Lifeskills
Home / School

For ages 9-up

Carole Marsh's
CURRICULUM LAB

OUTBREAKS, EPIDEMICS, & PANDEMICS—Including the Worldwide COVID-19 Pandemic
For ages 9-up
Copyright 2021, Carole Marsh Longmeyer
All rights reserved.

Current Edition ©April 2021

Illustrations by CJ Ellison, www.cjellisonart.com

Photograph credits:
Cover: Centers for Disease Control; Back cover: Sylvia Harrow; A Word from the Author (and other author photos): Sylvia Harrow; Page 18: Centers for Disease Control; Page 31: Wikipedia; Page 33: wallpaperflare.com; Page 38: Centers for Disease Control; Page 40: World Health Organization; Page 45: Bigstockphoto.com; Page 46: James Gathany, Immunization Action Coalition; Page 49: Public domain; Page 50: commons.wikimedia.org; Page 51: Wikipedia; Page 55: Public domain; Page 61: Public domain; Page 73: Wikipedia; Page 74: commons.wikimedia.org; Page 75: Wikipedia; commons.wikimedia.org; Page 76: commons.wikimedia.org; www.blackthen.com; Page 77: commons.wikimedia.org; Wikipedia; Page 78: www.digiralcommonwealth.org; Wikipedia; Page 79: commons.wikimedia.org

Germwise logo by Mark Dean, Gallopade International
Design and Paste-up by Tracy Uch
Videos by Studious Studios

Published by CAROLE MARSH'S CURRICULUM LAB

Distributed by GALLOPADE INTERNATIONAL
Carole Marsh Germwise Books

Available from Gallopade International via gallopade.com

AUTHOR AWARDS & AFFILIATIONS:
Go to authorcarolemarshlongmeyer.com

First Printing, 2021, USA

This book is NOT REPRODUCIBLE.

For further information, contact gallopade.com.

A PORTION OF THE PROCEEDS OF GERMWISE PRODUCTS WILL BE DONATED TO ORGANIZATIONS THAT HELP KIDS GET VACCINES.

BOOKS BY CAROLE MARSH

THE OFFICIAL GUIDE TO GERMS

A KID'S OFFICIAL GUIDE TO GERMS

505 FLABBERGASTING FACTS ABOUT GERMS

HOT ZONES OF AMERICA

OUTBREAKS, EPIDEMICS, & PANDEMICS—Including the Worldwide COVID-19 Pandemic

Table of Contents

A Word from the Author 7

PART ONE: An Overview of Pandemics—Today & Yesterday 9

    Something Germy This Way Comes! 10

    A Germy Glossary 11

    A Little History Might be in Order? 12

    Pandemics from the Historical Past 13

    Where Humans Go, Germs Go! 14

    The Geography of COVID-19 15

    The Old Versus the New 16

    BUT FIRST…The New Virus Hunters! 17

    SMALLPOX, a Big Deal! 18

    The Great Plague 19

    Cholera Comes Calling! 20

    A Candy Store of Diseases 21

    Childhood Diseases…You'll Be Glad You Didn't Have! 23

    Germs, Always the Germs! 24

    Are You Getting the Big Pandemic Picture? 25

    Babes in the New World Woods 26

PART TWO: More About Disease, Please! 27

    Do You Know About Disease? 28

    Do You Know the Meaning of These Germy Words? 29

    The Big Problem with Germs 30

    The Basics of Bacteria 31

    Viruses are Very Virulent 32

    Where Do Germs Come From? 33

    Are Germs Coming for Us? 34

Living with Germs Successfully: YOU CAN DO IT!	35
Your Amazing Immune System	36
Ready to Rumble!	36
Calling all T & B Cells	36
I Claim Immunity!	37
The CDC, the Place for Germs to Be!	38
Genetics & the Human Genome Project	39
The Human Genome Project	39
WHO?	40
PART THREE: I'm Sick! Now What?	**41**
AHHHHCHOOOO!	42
Antibodies & Antibiotics	43
Antibiotic Advice	43
Therapeutic Thoughts	44
Pets, Pregnancy, Other Populations, & COVID-19	45
Even Kids Helped Us Get a Vaccine!	46
PART FOUR: Examples of Outbreaks, Epidemics, & Pandemics	**47**
Ebola Outbreak, 2014-2016	48
Spanish Influenza Pandemic, 1917-1918	49
HIV & AIDS	50
COVID-19, 2020-???? Novel Coronavirus Pandemic	51
Off to a Bad Start / America Taken by Surprise / Pandemic, Panic, & Politics	51
Learning Curve / Heroes, Helpers…& Horrors / To Open or Close?	52
Ongoing Problems / Looking Ahead	53
It's a Small World, After All	54
Growing Up with Vaccines!	56

PART FIVE: LOOKING AHEAD: How Do We Get Out of This Mess?	**57**
Ongoing Pandemic Issues	58
Testing, Testing, One, Two, Three / Economic Considerations	58
Vulnerable Populations / The Unknown Unknowns	58
COVID Quarterbacking	59
The Endgame	60
Will COVID Ever End?	60
The Future	60
The Greatest Teachable Moment Ever!	62
COVID CALENDAR RECAP	**63**
COVID Calendar Recap	63
Career Opportunities Galore!	66
Heroes & Helpers	67
How You Can Help!	68
But Did They Use Novacaine?	69
DARPA: Infectious Disease Experts	70
Pandemics as the Impetus to Invention!	71
MORE GERMWISE HEROES & HELPERS THROUGHOUT HISTORY	**72**
GLOSSARY	**83**
Bibliography for Students	84
Germy Stuff to Read for Fun!	85
Acknowledgements	86
Index	87
About the Author	90

We're not in this Table of Contents!

But we're famous!

A Word from the Author...

Dear Kids,

Like you, I was minding my own business at the start of the year 2020. My rescue pup, Coconut, and I had been in Asheville, North Carolina for the holidays. (Coconut does not think much of snow!) In mid-February, we returned to our home in Beaufort, South Carolina. We had a lot of work, fun, and a few trips planned. We were looking forward to spring and summer—vacation, the beach, and things pretty much like they always were. And then, the whole world changed!

When I first heard about COVID-19, I got cold chills. Over the years, I had written a lot about germs. Anything that sounded like a "new" viral infection spooked me. Anything that had the words *bat, contagious,* or *pandemic* associated with it, outright scared me. Didn't such things always happen somewhere else? Sometimes, but this highly infectious coronavirus was heading *our way*. And, unlike the flu (which was still going around in early 2020) there was no vaccine or cure for this novel (new) coronavirus.

However, I was not too worried. After all, we had WHO, the World Health Organization. We have the CDC, the Centers for Disease Control. Surely, we were ready for anything that might come our way—if it really did come our way. Right?

You know the rest of the story! COVID-19 did come to America! The United States was not quite as ready to respond to a pandemic as we might have thought. We sure were not prepared (or happy) to leave school, stay home, wonder what might happen next, and worry.

Now we know that we need to be GERMWISE all our lives! We can hope there will never be another pandemic. In the meantime, we can learn how and why such a thing happens, and how we can plan and protect ourselves—today and tomorrow.

Let's start now!

Carole Marsh

PART ONE
An Overview of Pandemics—Today & Yesterday

WHAT JUST HAPPENED?

Hey, isn't an outbreak of disease uncommon?

Isn't it rare for it to turn into an epidemic, much less a pandemic?

Aren't pandemics something that happened long ago…in countries far away?

Good questions! Let's learn some answers.

Something Germy This Way Comes!

In early 2020, we began to see and hear news of an outbreak of a disease in Wuhan, China. Diseases are common and outbreaks happen all the time. But pretty soon we learned that this outbreak might be different.

In America, we were busy heading into the last few months of the school year. People were at work. Some places were still snowy, while others were already having spring warm-up. The annual flu season was on the wind down. And China seemed very far away.

As the news cycled—on television, in newspapers, and online—people began to talk about this disease being new, very contagious, and deadly; some of us paid attention. When photos of bats in Wuhan food markets were said to have been where the disease started, we thought one thing: *"Ewwwwww!"* When elderly people began to die of the disease, we felt bad. But China still seemed very far away.

Soon, there was news of the spread of this strange new virus in other Chinese towns. Before long, the virus spread across China's borders to other countries. The virus was given a long name soon shortened to COVID-19. When infected travelers showed up on cruise ships and airplanes, we began to worry. It's a small world, after all. And COVID-19 had no cure.

Hmmm…

©Carole Marsh / Carole Marsh's Curriculum Lab

A Germy Glossary

While it might seem odd to have the glossary at the front of this book, if you learn a few words and terms, it will help you understand the rest of the story a lot faster and a lot better. Let's go for it!

disease: an illness; often caused by a germ or microbe

bacteria: microscopic, one-celled living organisms; some are good, some bad

virus: an organism much smaller than bacteria that invades cells

pathogen: the germ or microbe that causes a disease

vector: the original source of a disease, such as a bat

index case: the first person known to get a specific disease

outbreak: the sudden occurrence of a disease

epidemic: the rapid spreading of a disease

pandemic: a worldwide epidemic or outbreak of disease

immune: protection against a disease

vaccine: a medication that can create immunity to a disease

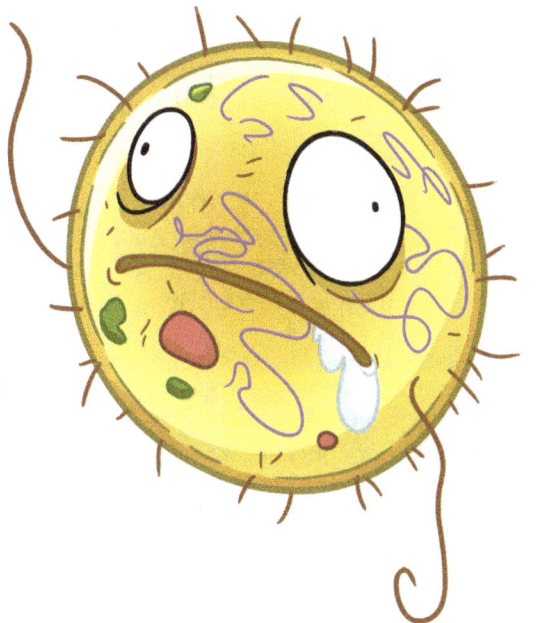

So...*bacteria* and *viruses* can infect you. You might get a *disease*. If you have had a *vaccine* against a disease, you probably won't get it because you'll be *immune* to it. If there is an *outbreak* of a disease and it spreads, it can create an *epidemic*. If the disease jumps the border of a country where it began, it may grow into a *pandemic*.

Got it? Good! Let's move on!

A Little History Might be in Order?

Have there been pandemics in the past? Oh, yes!

Some germs are a lot like tourists—they love to travel! Take a germ that usually sleeps deep in the rainforest. Let it get stuck on the sole of a boot of an anthropologist. Then let this person hop on an airplane and fly halfway around the world. A new germ in a new place. This would be a germ that people may have no immunity to. If you get infected by that germ, you may get very sick. If the disease spreads, well, you could end up with a pandemic.

Talk about a lesson in current events: In 2020 (perhaps even earlier) a real, live PANDEMIC showed up at America's front door! While we may never know exactly how it got here, or where the first case occurred, one thing was certain: it was here to stay!

The first cases in the United States most likely:

- came to New York City with passengers aboard international flights, or cruise ships from other countries.
- came to California, perhaps the same way, and infected an individual, and later a lot of elderly people in a nursing home.

Even while doctors, the government, hospitals, governors, and others were trying to figure out what was happening and what best to do about it, the infection spread rapidly and the number of cases increased.

Pretty soon, hospitals in some places (especially New York City) were filling up their emergency rooms and ICUs (Intensive Care Units) with those infected with COVID-19. Many of these patients died.

IS THIS HOW MOST PANDEMICS START?

Oh, yes. The germs know what they are doing. They are doing what germs do. That they are invisible does not help anything. That a person can be infected and not have any symptoms (be *asymptomatic*) does not help. Why? Because in the meantime, they are going about their everyday activities, possibly infecting others.

I guess Sherlock Holmes said it best: *"THE GAME IS ON!"*

Pandemics have happened before and will happen again. It's how we respond to them—especially how fast and effectively—that makes all the difference in the world.

Pandemics from the Historical Past

Let's look at a list of some of the outbreaks, epidemics, and pandemics that happened long ago. As you see, the world has been plagued by plagues since the earliest times.

NAME	DATE	TYPE	DEATH TOLL
Antonine Plague	165-180 BCE	Smallpox or measles	5 million
Japanese Epidemic	735-737 BCE	Smallpox virus	1 million
Justinian Plague	541-542 BCE	Bacterial	30-50 million
Black Death	1347-1351 CE	Bacterial	200 million
New World Smallpox	1520 CE-on	Viral	56 million
Great Plague, London	1665 CE	Bacterial	100,000
Italian Plague	1629-1631 CE	Bacterial	1 million
Cholera Pandemics	1817-1923 CE	Bacterial	1 million+
Third Plague	1885 CE	Bacterial	12 million
Yellow Fever	Late 1800s	Viral	100,000-150,000
Russian Flu	1889-1890	Viral	1 million

This list is of only some pandemics over the years, the more deadly ones. But outbreaks and epidemics are not uncommon. In fact, they can occur almost anywhere, at any time. All do not reach the category of pandemic, thank goodness.

However, as people in small hunting and gathering tribes shifted to more agrarian (farming) communities, there was more opportunity for people and animals to interact. And so, there were more chances for germs to jump from animals to humans and create more epidemics.

As civilization advanced, larger cities, trade across nations and seas, and more interactions between people, animals, and ecosystems created an almost constant guarantee for germ spread, epidemics, outbreaks, and pandemics.

Today, we struggle with how to learn from past pandemics, implement new strategies, and respond quickly to help stop an outbreak from getting away from us.

BCE: Before the Common Era
CE: Common Era

Where Humans Go, Germs Go!

Here is a list of some pandemics which have occurred more recently, or are ongoing.

NAME	DATE	TYPE	DEATH TOLL, WORLDWIDE
Spanish Flu	1918-1919	Viral	40-50 million
Asian Flu	1957-1958	Viral	1.1 million
Hong Kong Flu	1968-1970	Viral	1 million
HIV/AIDS	1981-now	Viral	25-35 million
Swine Flu	2009-2010	Viral	200,000
SARS	2002-2003	Coronavirus	770
Ebola	2014-2016	Viral	11,000
MERS	2015-now	Coronavirus	850
COVID-19	2019-now	Coronavirus	Approx. 1 million (as of Dec. 2020)

By 1900 there was a larger worldwide population and increased travel between countries. Germs did not stay in their place of origin. They hitched a ride on humans and traveled the world, creating ever more opportunities for infection from highly contagious diseases. The current COVID-19 pandemic is a good example of this.

Diseases that started as an outbreak, but led to an epidemic or pandemic, include malaria, tuberculosis, leprosy, smallpox, and in more recent times, HIV/AIDS, Ebola, and a number of new coronaviruses, including COVID-19.

The Geography of COVID-19

- It started in Wuhan, **China**. In December 2019, WHO reported a cluster of cases of pneumonia in Wuhan, Hubei Province. The cause was later determined to be a novel coronavirus, meaning a new virus not seen before. In January 2020, WHO began to monitor the outbreak and warn all nations about the threat of a new coronavirus.

- In January 2020, the first case of COVID-19 was recorded in **Thailand**; the virus had spread outside of China.

- By January 30, WHO reported 7,818 cases, with 82 of these being in 18 countries outside of China.

- In March, WHO declared the outbreak a *pandemic*, meaning worldwide in scope. As the highly contagious virus spread, more countries were affected.

FLOATING COUNTRIES: When the outbreak came, most people were living their ordinary lives. However, thousands of people were aboard cruise ships all around the world. These people were from different countries. Once some of them tested positive for COVID, the infection often moved quickly from passenger to passenger in such close quarters.

FLYING COUNTRIES: The same was true of airplanes. As people boarded a flight in one nation and flew to another, they took more than their luggage; they brought their germs with them. Like a cruise ship, the close confines of an aircraft made infection more likely.

It is easy to see how the virus spread so rapidly even while we were just learning it existed, what it was, how it spread, and how to protect ourselves.

Soon COVID-19 would be found on every continent except **Antarctica**.

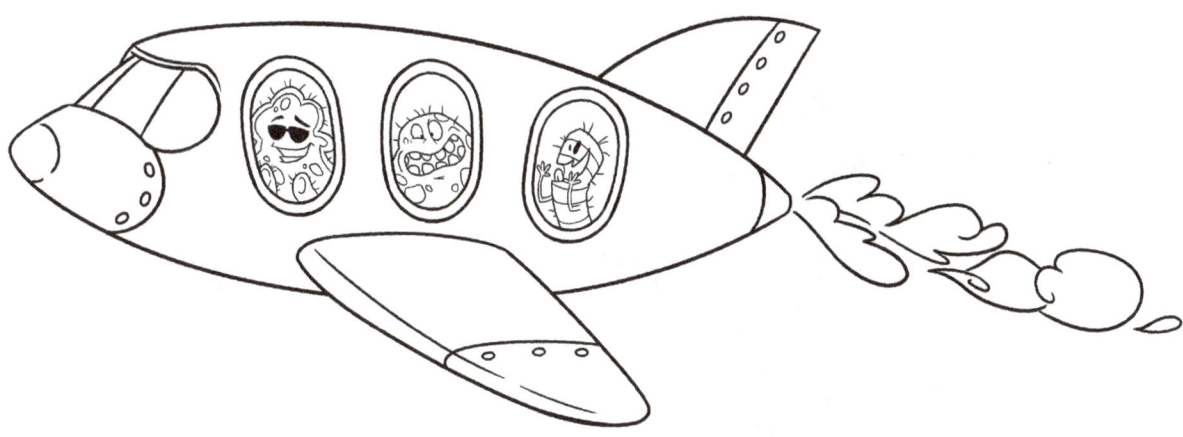

©Carole Marsh / Carole Marsh's Curriculum Lab

The Old Versus the New

Whenever a new disease infected a human, they wondered, *"How did that happen? Where did that come from?"*

In ancient societies, people believed that gods and spirits sent diseases as a punishment. However, as early as 541 BCE, people were able to trace the origin of a plague back to the country where it started. They also figured out that it spread through trade routes. In spite of this realization, some people blamed outbreaks on leaders, such as Justinian, God, or almost anything or anyone else.

Despite such ignorance or stubbornness, over time people began to learn more about disease and how to reduce death rates. Of course, nothing was more helpful than advances in healthcare, antibiotics, vaccines, and other medical strategies.

> **quarantine:** *a period of time when a person (animal or product) must be isolated to ensure they are not infected with a disease*

As long ago as the 14th century, people learned to practice *quarantine* to help slow the spread of disease. The port of Venice in Italy required ships coming from infected ports to sit offshore at anchor for 40 days before landing. In fact, the word quarantine comes from the Italian term *quaranta giorni,* or 40 days.

As time went by, savvy observers began to track some diseases back to their specific source. They used data to help discern the particular source of an outbreak. Scientists learned to track infections to make predictions about the probable spread of a disease.

Even though we have much more information, global communication, and better disease tracking skills, COVID-19 has shown that we can still be too slow in our early reporting of and reaction to an outbreak to reduce the infection, spread, and death toll as much as we might want.

It takes a lot of planning and practice to prevent an outbreak from becoming an epidemic or, worse yet, a full-blown pandemic.

Let's see how others have tackled this challenge in the past.

©Carole Marsh / Carole Marsh's Curriculum Lab

BUT FIRST...The New Virus Hunters!

As you will see, in the past it was difficult to even ponder the questions,

**HOW DID THIS HAPPEN?
WHERE DID IT COME FROM?**

After all, without microscopes, they could not SEE the germs.

Today, we still cannot see the germs, but we know they are there. We know where they come from. And we know how "this happened." The Big Question today is: HOW DO WE AVOID THIS IN THE FUTURE?!

Working on the answers are crucial VIRUS HUNTERS. These scientists don hazmat suits, take portable labs, and travel the world. They march into jungles to find caves filled with bats, for example.

Virus hunter in the jungle.

They catch the bats in harp traps (that do not hurt the bats) and take blood, urine, fecal, and other samples to test and see what pathogens different bats have inside them. These pathogens do not hurt the bats, but if they spillover to humans via food, air, a cut in our skin—however they are transmitted—a NEW outbreak can occur. As we know, this can turn into a deadly pandemic.

"If we know which animals harbor which pathogens, we have a head start on keeping animals and humans apart," explains one virus hunter. "If we build a library of animal viruses ahead of time, we will be better able to tackle a new outbreak when an emergence occurs."

FACT-ERIA!

Close to Home!

Virus hunters also search America for dangerous pathogens. Some deer harbor a microbe that causes CWD, Chronic Wasting Disease. We would not want that germ to jump to humans!

Where else might you find Virus Hunters?

USAMRIID=U.S. Army Medical Research Institute of Infectious Diseases

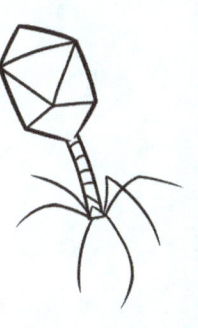

©Carole Marsh / Carole Marsh's Curriculum Lab

SMALLPOX, a Big Deal!

There have been numerous smallpox epidemics over the course of history.

Smallpox is caused by the viruses *Variola major* or *Variola minor*. It is an infectious disease. Early symptoms include fever and vomiting. Next, a skin rash and sores in the mouth occur. In a few days, the rash turns into fluid-filled bumps with a dent in the center that scab over, fall off, and leave scars. The high death rate was about 30% higher in babies. Many who survived were left blind.

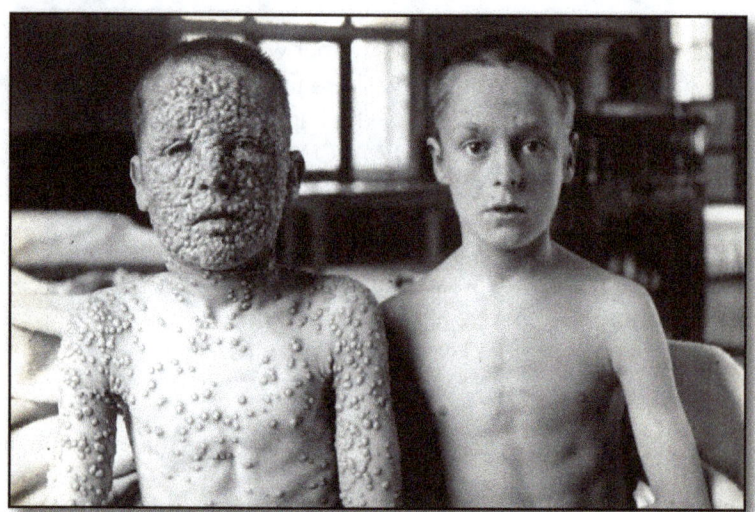
One brother got the vaccine; the other did not.

Yes, smallpox is a horrid disease. It was also known as the *pox*, *speckled monster*, and *red plague*. There was no cure. Where did it come from? Scientists have found evidence of smallpox in 3rd century mummies in Egypt. Outbreaks over the years killed many people. In the 20th century, possibly 300 million people still died of smallpox.

Inoculations for smallpox started in China as early as the 1500s. In 1796, Edward Jenner created the first modern smallpox vaccine. Even then, around 500 million people died of the disease. In spite of intensive smallpox inoculation programs, 15 million cases still occurred a year up until 1967.

Nonetheless, smallpox is one of the infectious diseases deemed to have been eradicated from the earth. The last case in the United States was seen in 1949. Vaccinations were stopped in 1972. There are only 15 million doses of vaccine available.

plague = pronounced **PLAYGUH**
bubonic = pronounced **BOO BON ICK**
pneumonic = pronounced **NEW MON ICK**
buboes = pronounced **BOO BOWS***

*the name of the pus-filled boils on the skin of a smallpox victim

©Carole Marsh / Carole Marsh's Curriculum Lab

The Great Plague

An epidemic of plague, called the Black Death, spread across Europe during the Middle Ages. From the 1200s to the 1800s, the disease was spread by the now rare black rat. The rat transmitted infected fleas to people. The fleas were infected with *Yersinia pestis*, a deadly microorganism.

Bubonic Plague: spreads from the bite of infected rat fleas; the disease causes swollen glands called buboes in the neck, armpit, and groin.

Pneumonic Plague: spreads through coughing and affects the lungs.

This Great Plague lasted from 1346-1353. It spread from Central and East Asia along the Silk Road of spice trading, on the rats aboard merchant ships, and on to Africa, Western Asia, Europe, and around the world.

It is now believed that once the rats came ashore via ships and fleas they spread pneumonic plague across land. Possibly 200 million people died from these diseases, the deadliest pandemic (recorded to-date) in human history.

Millions of people died during several waves of epidemics. This plague was not caused by a virus. It was caused by a bacterium. The bacterium that caused the plague was not identified until 1894. A vaccine was developed two years later.

During the Great Plague of London in 1665, more than one-third of the city's half-million people died of the disease. In the 1900s, an outbreak of the plague hit San Francisco, California, on the western coast of the United States. In the 1960s and 1970s, the country of Vietnam was a hotbed of plague. A 1994 outbreak killed around 800 people in Surat, India.

In the 17th century, before people had any idea what caused this dreaded disease, they carried pouches filled with sweet-smelling herbs or flowers in hopes of keeping the plague at bay.

When there were not enough coffins for the dead, lead crosses were placed on the victims instead.

©Carole Marsh / Carole Marsh's Curriculum Lab

Cholera Comes Calling!

feces: *human excrement, waste; poop*

cholera: *pronounced CAH LA RAH*

The first major cholera epidemic occurred in the country of India in the early 1800s. Cholera reached the United States in 1832 via sailors and immigrants. The famous 1854 cholera outbreak in London, England, was stopped when traced to a contaminated public water pump. Major cholera outbreaks have occurred in many places around the world including America and Canada. A 1991 epidemic in Peru spread through Latin America, killing 11,000. A 2016 outbreak in Yemen continued into 2020. Over the years, millions have died from cholera.

Cholera is an infection of the small intestine. It is caused by water contaminated with the *Vibrio cholerae* bacterium. In places where water is contaminated by human feces, the microbes that cause cholera can breed rapidly. Once a person is infected, the bacteria multiply in the intestines and release toxins. Symptoms include vomiting and diarrhea. Countries where poverty and slums are common continue to have cholera outbreaks. Cholera can also break out following a natural disaster, when people may be exposed to contaminated drinking water. A vaccine can give protection for a short time.

Cholera pandemics have plagued people even until the present, with a cumulative death toll in the millions. In 1961, a new strain of the disease emerged in Indonesia and still spreads in developing countries. In the 1990s, some scientists warned of a worrisome resistance to drugs used to treat cholera.

While improved sanitation is crucial to avoiding cholera outbreaks, other factors play a role in the ongoing spread of the disease. These can include war, refugee camps, damaged sanitation systems during hurricanes and other disasters, the eating of contaminated seafood and fish, famine, lack of handwashing (or clean water to do so), lack of health services, and more.

Cholera is not contagious, but it continues to plague people around the world.

FACT-ERIA!
A human bowel movement has nearly 100 billion bacteria per gram of wet stool.

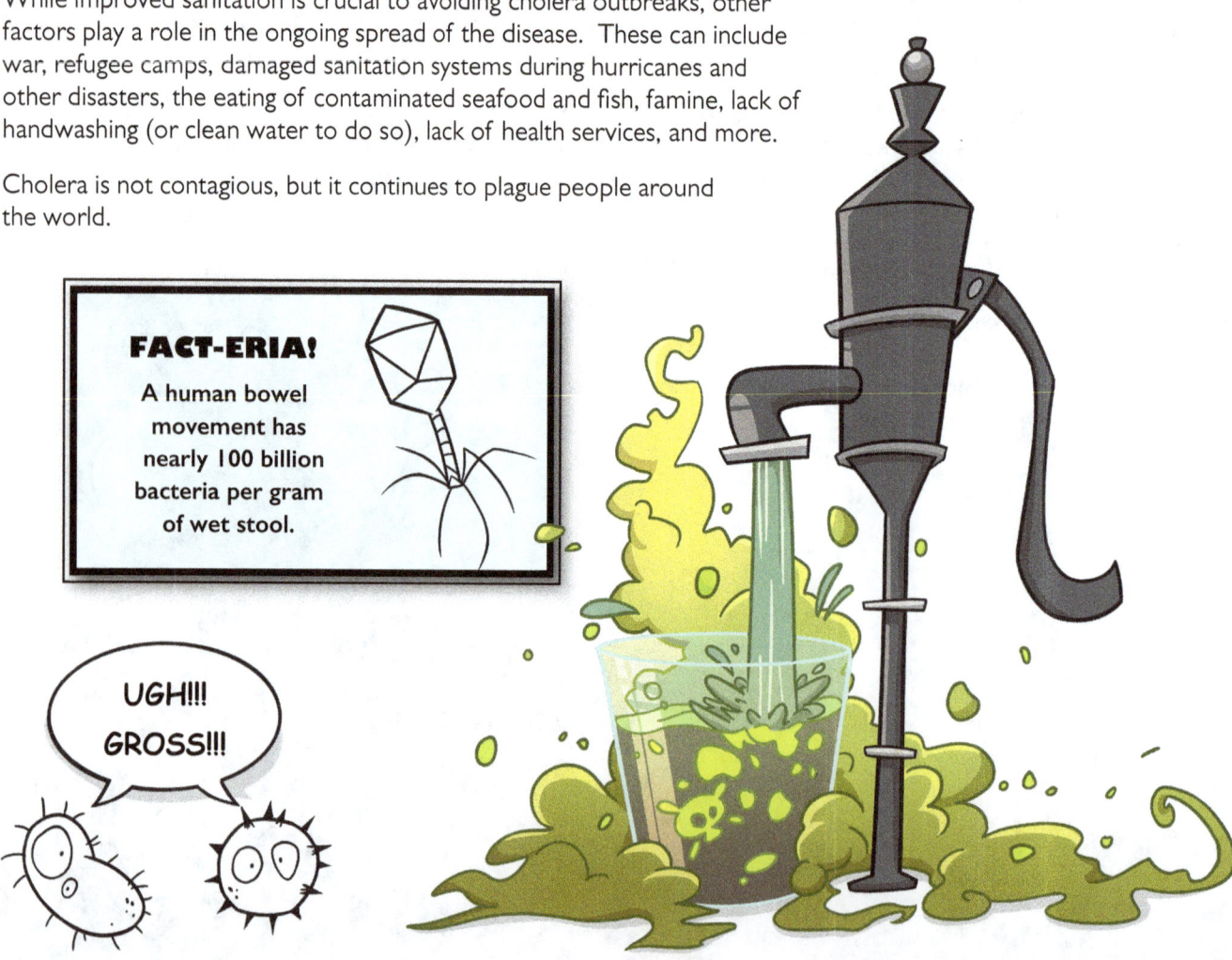

UGH!!! GROSS!!!

©Carole Marsh / Carole Marsh's Curriculum Lab

A Candy Store of Diseases

Before we leave Part One, let's look at a few other pandemic-worthy diseases. There are many more diseases than we can cover, but here are a few significant ones.

HIV/AIDS

AIDS=Acquired Immune Deficiency Syndrome
It is caused by HIV=Human Immunodeficiency Virus

HIV and AIDS had gotten the attention of doctors long before the 1980s when an outbreak swept across the United States and the rest of the world. There was a lot of initial shock and controversy over this disease because it primarily infected homosexual (gay) men. Once infected, a man could spread the disease to other men, women, and even children. People can also get infected by using needles that have infected blood on them. The virus attacks the immune system, destroying so many cells that the body can't fight infection. There is no cure, but today there is an effective treatment. Around 70 million people have been infected with HIV. About 35 million have died from the disease since the start of the epidemic.

ANTHRAX

Anthrax occurs naturally in the environment. The word anthrax comes from the Greek word for coal, *anthrakis*. It can be found in soil. People who work with animal hides are sometimes exposed to anthrax. Anthrax was a disease of Roman farm animals. At one time American soldiers were inoculated against anthrax since it was a possible bio-warfare agent. In 2001, letters containing anthrax were mailed to people in the U.S. Some were infected and died.

LEPROSY

Leprosy is an example of an ancient disease. Leprosy is mostly called Hansen's Disease today. It is believed to be one of the oldest diseases and occurred most during the Middle Ages. While it is not highly contagious, rare, and usually found in remote places, there are still about six million cases today. About 5,000 people in the U.S. have leprosy. However, many of us have leprosy antibodies because we may have been exposed to the bacterium. There are anti-leprosy drugs, but if untreated the disease can cause severe facial distortion and even the loss of fingers, toes, ears, or nose.

MALARIA

Known as the disease of the jungle, malaria is caused by a single-cell organism contracted through the bite of an infected mosquito. Malaria was common in soldiers who fought on islands in the Pacific Ocean during World War II. At least 500 million cases of malaria worldwide are recorded each year. Quinine, from the bark of cinchona trees, has long been used to treat malaria. Where there are a lot of mosquitoes, people also use insect repellent, wear long pants and sleeves, put mosquito netting over beds, and may take anti-malarial drugs.

POLIO

Poliomyelitis (called polio) first appeared in prehistory. It was not until the 1900s when epidemics occurred in Europe and the United States. The disease became a regular event during summer months. In the 1940s and 1950s, polio would paralyze or kill more than half a million people around the world each year. Polio was once a petrifying disease to families who had no idea what caused it. When one of their children contracted polio, they sometimes brought them to a treatment center and left them, fearing their other children might get infected. Victims of polio were often put into what was called an "iron lung" which breathed for them. Eventually, a successful vaccine was developed. Polio has almost been eradicated around the world. U.S. President Franklin D. Roosevelt contracted polio as an adult and was permanently paralyzed from the waist down. He established a rehabilitation center in Warm Springs, Georgia, which still exists. Polio was one of the first diseases where a cure was aided by fund-raising groups such as the March of Dimes. Shriners Hospitals for Children treated any child with polio free of charge. Those who survived polio as adults were active in the disability rights movement that have helped many disabled people. There are 10-20 million polio survivors around the world, including about 250,000 in the United States.

TUBERCULOSIS

Tuberculosis is an infectious disease caused by bacteria that usually affects the lungs. Most infections show no symptoms. Untreated, about half of infections lead to death. The disease can be spread from people with active "TB" when they cough, spit, speak, or sneeze. There is a vaccine against tuberculosis and drug treatments for those who contract it. This disease goes back to ancient times, even being found in Egyptian mummies. People who have TB are sometimes confined to tuberculosis sanitariums.

TYPHOID

Typhoid Fever is a bacterial infection caused by a specific kind of salmonella. Symptoms include fever and a skin rash with rose-colored spots. You get typhoid by eating or drinking food or water contaminated with the feces of an infected person. (And now you know yet another good reason to wash your hands before you eat!) There is a vaccine. The disease is most common among children in India. There are still about 400 cases in the United States each year. The chlorination of drinking water has helped to reduce instances of the disease. During World War I, the entire U.S. Army was immunized against typhoid, saving many lives. "Typhoid Mary" was a cook in New York City who had to be quarantined to keep her from infecting people.

©Carole Marsh / Carole Marsh's Curriculum Lab

Childhood Diseases...
You'll Be Glad You Didn't Have!

As you have learned in this overview of historic pandemics, many diseases have been very hard on children. We will end Part One with a look at so-called "childhood diseases" that we are so fortunate to have vaccines for today. While we might not like to get our "shots" at the pediatrician or health department, that is a lot better than getting these diseases. (I know—I had most of them!) Some are caused by viruses; others by bacteria. Most of these diseases are very contagious. When you get a vaccine at the right age, you can usually skip that disease and be immune to it for life.

Measles: Very contagious! Can quickly pass through a classroom or a school. Caused by the measles virus. Lasts about 7-10 days. Symptoms=high fever, cough, runny nose, red eyes, and a red rash over much of your body. It's no fun to be out of school when you feel so bad. Girls, you won't want to look in the mirror! Measles is also very dangerous for women who are pregnant.

Mumps: It's a funny name, but there's nothing funny about this viral disease that is very contagious. You may have fever, headache, muscle aches, tiredness, and a loss of appetite. But even worse, your salivary glands will swell so that you look like a chipmunk! Your cheeks and neck will be very sore and tender. Mumps last about two weeks.

Chickenpox: No one likes the sound of any disease with the word "pox" in it. Chickenpox is caused by a virus that gives you a red, itchy rash on your face, back, chest, and pretty much any place it wants to go. The blisters burst and scab over. The worse thing is that you are not supposed to scratch them. If you do, they may get infected or leave scars.

Diphtheria: A serious disease caused by bacteria that makes a type of toxin (poison) that can make it hard to breathe, affect your heart, cause paralysis, and even death. Fortunately, there is a vaccine for this disease, which is now not so common in the United States. You can get it when someone who has it coughs or sneezes, by sharing drinks, or (yikes!) kissing!

Scarlet Fever: This bacterial illness can develop when you have strep throat. Symptoms include a bright red rash that covers most of your body, a sore throat, and high fever. It can be treated with antibiotics.

Whooping Cough: A very contagious disease that affects the respiratory tract. It is very dangerous for babies. You may have a runny nose and bad cough that makes a "whooping" sound.

An important thing to remember about "childhood" diseases is that most can affect infants, children, and even young adults. This is another reason that getting the right vaccines at the right time is good for your health.

©Carole Marsh / Carole Marsh's Curriculum Lab

Germs, Always the Germs!

Here are examples of other germs that have plagued us. This list gets added to all the time.

Kuru: This curious disease still exists in only one place in the world—Papua, New Guinea. From around 1950 to 1970, more than 3,000 of the Fore people who live here died from what they called "laughing disease." The Fore are cannibals. They honor their dead by eating them, especially their brains, which they consider a delicacy. Since the women of the tribe prepared these meals, about eight times more of them died than the men in the tribe. The cause of this disease is a *prion*, a single protein that can cause infection. Because prions are a natural part of the body, our immune system does not recognize these prions as a danger. These deadly prions can lurk in the body and cause a sudden deadly disease in the future.

Mad Cow: This is the nickname for the disease *Bovine Spongiform Encephalopathy*. It is also caused by prions. It can infect the brain and spinal cord of cattle, which eventually kills them. In rare cases, humans can get a form of Mad Cow called *variant Creutzfeldt-Jakob* (pronounced YAKOB) disease, which is also fatal.

Ebola: This disease is a hemorrhagic fever caused by the Ebola virus. It was first discovered in 1976 near the Ebola River in the Democratic Republic of Congo in Africa. Ebola is an example of a disease that can spread from an animal, such as a monkey or bat, to humans. Ebola outbreaks are always frightening because the disease has no cure and causes a horrible "bleeding out" kind of death.

Swine Flu: In 2009 there was a swine flu pandemic. This is a type of influenza from the H1N1 virus, like the one that caused the Spanish Flu pandemic. This new strain of flu came from a combo of bird, swine (pig), and human flu viruses.

SARS: SARS stands for *Severe Acute Respiratory Syndrome*. It is caused by a type of coronavirus. In a 2002-2004 outbreak of this disease, scientists traced the source of the virus to cave-dwelling horseshoe bats. In 2019, a related strain may have caused COVID-19.

MERS: MERS stands for *Middle East Respiratory Syndrome*. It is also caused by a coronavirus. The disease first appeared in an outbreak in Saudi Arabia in 2012, although it originated in the country of Jordan. There was a later outbreak in the nation of Korea. The disease can infect anyone from ages 1-to-100. It is transmitted through close contact with an infected person.

COVID-19: In 2019, a novel (new) type of coronavirus was identified. It soon blossomed from a start in China to other countries and then around the world to create the latest global pandemic. As cases and deaths continue to rise, cities, states, and countries try to learn about and cope with this deadly viral disease. It is unknown when this disease will come to an end, if you can get infected again and again, or when enough vaccine will become available and distributed widely enough to end the pandemic.

Are You Getting the Big Pandemic Picture?

The purpose of Part One is to help you see that COVID-19 (our current pandemic) is just one in a long list of diseases that have plagued people over time. And, that if history continues like it has so far, we will always have outbreaks of disease that lead to epidemics and sometimes pandemics.

You may feel dismayed, but don't be too discouraged. Over time, we have learned more and more about diseases: what causes them; how to identify them; how to create vaccines against some of them; medications and treatments that help, and much more—including how to cure a few of them.

However, to be honest, diseases have another kind of curious history. The history of disease, as you have read, is sad and bad, includes illness, death, disfigurement and all kinds of truly horrible outcomes. But another consistent fact about disease is that people often do not react wisely or well. We can see this today (with COVID-19) when people know that social distancing helps a lot, but they still gather on the beach in large groups, crowd into bars, or celebrate at big family gatherings. In many ways, we do not act any smarter than the ancient Greeks or others who knew quarantine was a good thing, but avoided it like, well, like the plague. Even very long ago, people learned that masks were helpful, yet, for one reason or ten others, they refused to wear one.

Also, long ago, people spent a lot of time arguing about what, or who, caused a disease. Blaming others did not help anything. Leaders have been weak and ineffective in past plagues, and today we see politics often seeming to be more important that scientific facts. That does not help either. As I did my research, I was very dismayed to see that some people in the past (even in America during the Spanish Flu epidemic) actually lied about the disease, the facts, the numbers of infected and dead. So, it is sad for me to have to say that adults do not always act very responsibly during a time when speed, smarts, wisdom, good decisions and more are VERY IMPORTANT in any disease outbreak. It is life or death, after all.

In summary, a PANDEMIC is a terrible thing, and scary. The germs do not care about us. It does not help that they are invisible, because if we could see them, we would stay as far away as possible, right? But we can also see hero and helper doctors, EMS, nurses, and others. Scientists around the world work day and night to find a cure, vaccine, or whatever may help our COVID-19 situation.

There is hope and help. The more we know and the more we learn, the better we (at any age) can make good choices, including perhaps, a future career that you may have never considered before now. That's exciting.

Pandemics are not boring, so let's keep going!

©Carole Marsh / Carole Marsh's Curriculum Lab

Babes in the New World Woods

When the first colonists came to the New World, many of them brought their children. It is said that they "feared not" the voyage nor this strange new land. One writer described happy girls and boys with rosy cheeks gathering wild strawberries and laughing. But, soon, winter came, "and death." The colonists had brought more than the things needed to start a new life. They brought germs, and germs brought death.

Even as households were established, crops planted, and new babies born, the colonists could not shake the incessant illnesses that especially infected infants and young children. "There is not a house where there is not one dead," mourned one father. Even prosperous colonies could not escape the menace of disease. Newborns were carted to church even in freezing temperatures to be baptized as soon as possible, in case death soon claimed them.

The mortality rate of babies was exceedingly high. Sometimes, they died one at a time; other times, they died in groups or even in vast numbers. What killed them? What parents and doctors called "putrid fevers, epidemic influenzas, malignant sore throats, and raging small pox." Disease. Why? Because no one knew to heed the laws of sanitation. Sanitizing was uncommon. And although they figured out that isolating sick children from well was a good idea, it was rarely possible in the close quarters where they struggled to stay warm.

The science of medicine was unknown, as was the cause of the horrid diseases. Quack medicines were common, such as "snail water," which generally did nothing or caused more harm. I mean, just how helpful could a vile concoction of "vipers, wine, opium" and even poisons actually be? For some sick children, the "cure" was dipping them head-first in icy water then leaving them undressed. If that did not work, taking blood out of their feet was tried. If a family could afford it, they might buy a necklace of wolf fangs to wear around the neck.

While we don't have all the cures we might wish today in the 21st century, we should be grateful how far we have come.—

Information for the story came from *Child Life in Colonial Days* by Alice Morse Earle

PART TWO
More About Disease, Please!

Now that we've looked a bit at major outbreaks, epidemics, and pandemics of the past—as well as a quick glance at the present: COVID-19—let's learn more about diseases to help it all make sense.

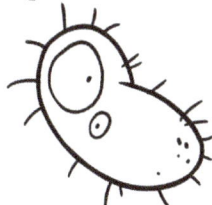

Should I get a vaccine?

I'll get one if you get one!

©Carole Marsh / Carole Marsh's Curriculum Lab

Do You Know About Disease?

We get a cold and say we are sick. We get the flu and say we are ill. But disease has a specific definition:

disease: *An abnormal condition of a part, organ, or system of an organism resulting from various causes, such as infection, inflammation, environmental factors, or genetic defect, and characterized by an identifiable group of signs, symptoms, or both.*

In this book we are talking about diseases that are caused by germs, diseases that spread, diseases that are infectious or contagious. A disease is definitely an illness. Not all diseases lead to outbreaks, epidemics, or pandemics, but many can. We say we are "plagued" by things like too much homework or rain every time there's a ballgame. But to be plagued with a genuine worldwide pandemic of a major disease such as the Bubonic Plague is an entirely different thing. A serious thing. A potentially deadly thing. The more we know and understand, the better we are able to ward off disease whenever possible.

Many diseases are caused by germs. This may be *viruses* or *bacteria*. We know that covering our mouth when we sneeze, washing our hands after we go to the bathroom, staying home from school when we have a cold, and other smart hygiene help us avoid getting infected by germs.

Many diseases are contagious and can spread in different ways:
- through the bites of infected mosquitoes, lice, fleas, and ticks, for example
- through close contact with infected animals or people
- through warm, damp environments where germs thrive

Building up an immunity to some germs can ward off some diseases. When we get our immunizations at the right age, we have helped ourselves avoid disease.

Nonetheless, in spite of knowledge, good hygiene, vaccines, and all our best efforts, most people end up getting sick or ill from disease at some time in their life. Keeping our immune system strong, knowing what early symptoms of different diseases are, and getting medical treatment fast, can help avoid some of the more serious misery of a disease.

What else can YOU do to help yourself stay safe from disease?
- Stay away from people who are sick when you can.
- Eat healthy, exercise, get enough rest, and practice good hygiene like regular and thorough handwashing.

Do You Know the Meaning of These Germy Words?

Now that you know a little more about disease, let's learn the simple, but specific, meaning of essential words to better understand germs.

germ: A microorganism that causes disease. Germs include bacteria, viruses, fungi, and protozoa.

bacteria: Tiny, one-celled creatures that get nutrients from their environment to live. (A single bacteria is called a bacterium.)

viruses: A microscopic microbe that can infect cells and cause a disease.

pathogen: A bacterium, virus, or other microorganism that can cause disease.

disease: The 4 main types are infectious, deficiency, hereditary, and physiological. Diseases can also be communicable or non-communicable. Pandemics generally involve infectious communicable diseases.

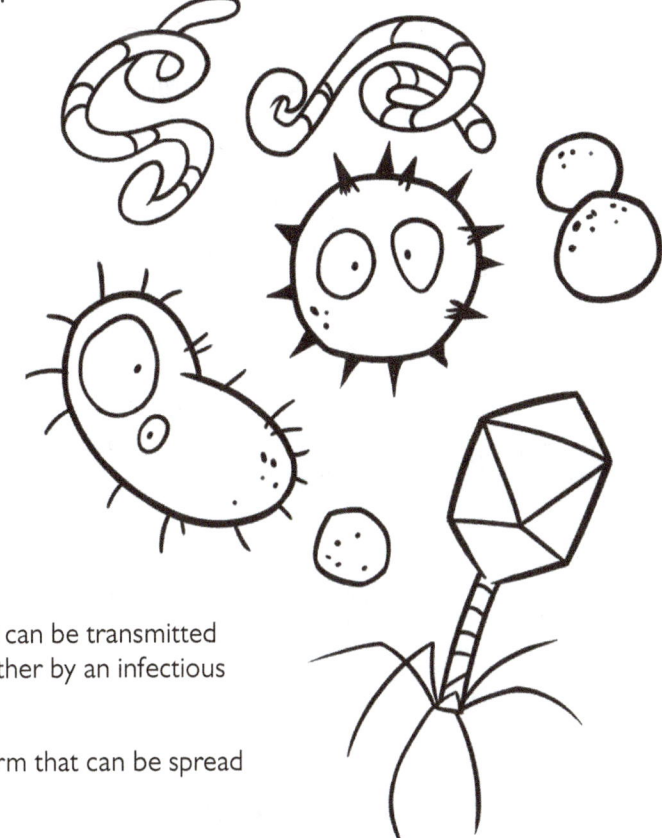

communicable: An infectious disease that can be transmitted directly or indirectly from one source to another by an infectious agent or its toxins.

infectious: A disease or disease-causing germ that can be spread from one person to another.

contagious: Spread from one person to another by direct contact or in some other way.

hygiene: Practices to maintain personal cleanliness and avoid illness.

immunity: Resistance to a certain type of disease.

vaccine: A substance that can provide a person immunity to a disease.

immunization: To make a person or animal immune to a specific disease.

inoculation: To be injected (or otherwise receive) a vaccine to give you immunity to a disease.

immune system: The cells, tissues, and organs that help your body fight infections and other diseases.

©Carole Marsh / Carole Marsh's Curriculum Lab

The Big Problem with Germs

The BIG problem with germs is that they are so tiny!
As you have probably figured out, they are invisible to what we call "the naked eye."

If we could actually see germs on our hands, face, or toilet seat, I think we would be champion handwashers!
But even though we can't see germs, we can't afford to ignore them.

Scientists can see germs, even the tiniest viruses, with microscopes. This was not always true, of course. Can you imagine that the first scientist to see germs beneath a microscope said, "Wow!" But what good is what scientists and doctors learn about germs...if WE don't pay attention?

Remember: Some germs are good; we could not live without them.
Bacteria are actually the dominate forms of life on Earth.
There are more germs than any other living organisms!

The human body contains TRILLIONS of microorganisms.
In fact, they outnumber human cells by 10-to-1.
Because they are so small, these microorganisms only make up 1-3 percent of a body's mass.
That means a 200-pound man would have about 2-6 pounds of bacteria!
But we need our good germs to be healthy.

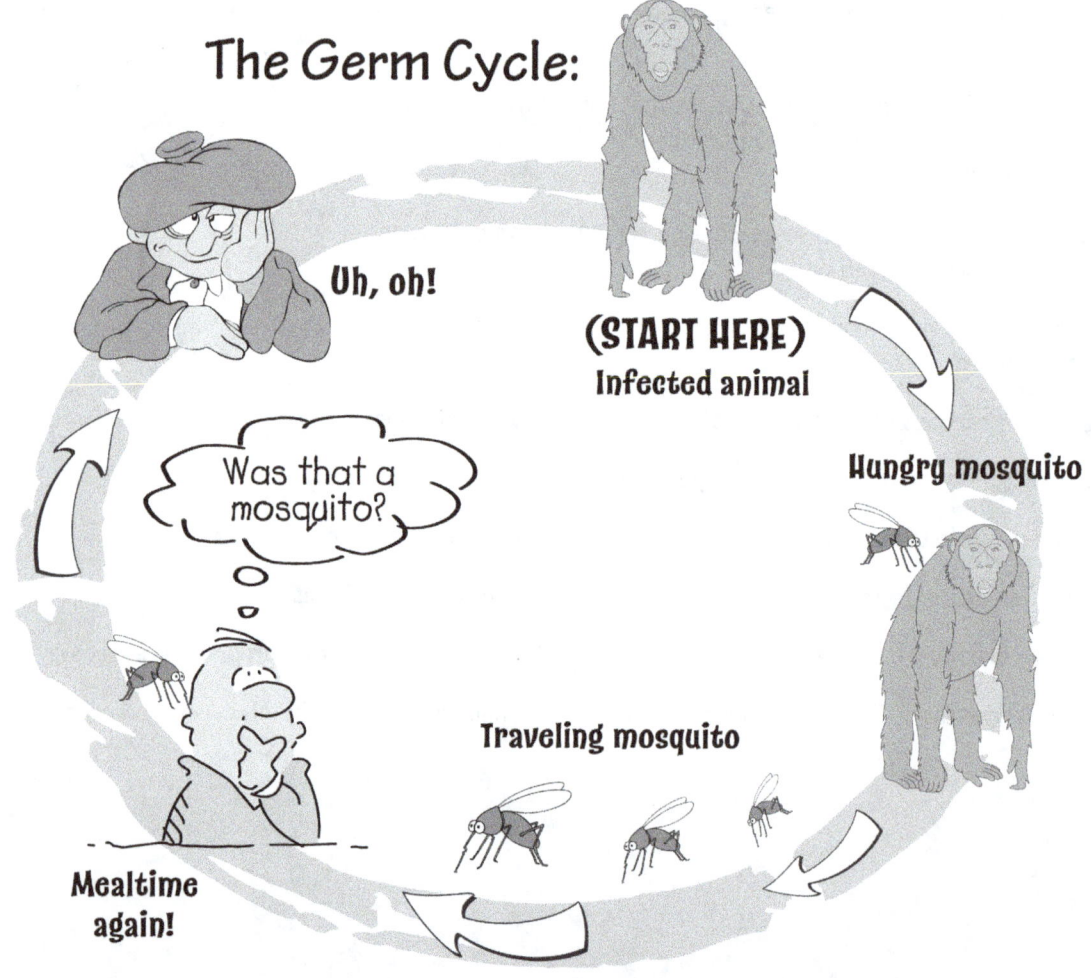

The Germ Cycle:

(START HERE) Infected animal
Hungry mosquito
Traveling mosquito
Mealtime again!
"Was that a mosquito?"
Uh, oh!

The Basics of Bacteria

We inhale and exhale bacteria. We eat and poop bacteria. Most bacteria are harmless. Billions of bacteria live in your mouth, stomach, and intestines. They stay busy destroying other harmful microbes.

A bacterium is a complete living cell. Bacteria are often highly-specialized. They thrive in optimum conditions but are unable to live and grow otherwise. Some bacteria cause disease by releasing toxins into the body. Other bacteria directly invade cells.

- Different types of bacteria target specific kinds of cells.
- Doctors use drugs such as antibiotics to combat bacteria.
- The overuse of drugs may cause bacteria to adapt, change, or mutate.
- This may cause them to be immune to some drugs.
- Drug immunity is not helpful when you are trying to fight germs!
- The scientific name for a bacteria cell is *prokaryotes*. These are considered simple cells since they do not contain a nucleus or any other specialized organelles. However they do have a tail, called a *flagellum*.
- Good bacteria in our gut include *lactococcus*, *lactobacillus*, and *lactobacillus bifidus*. These may aid digestion and break down the food we eat. Bacteria is used to make foods such as yogurt, cheese, soy sauce, and pickles. Yum!
- Bad bacteria include *clostridium perfringens*, *staphylococcus*, and *escherichia coli*.

FACT-ERIA!
How does the doctor determine which germ has attacked your body? The most accurate way is to analyze your symptoms and examine bacteria found in your mouth, urine, or feces.

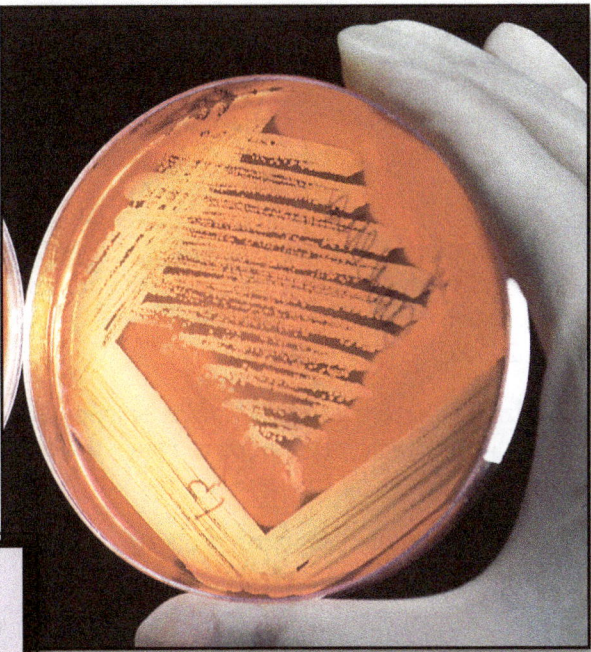

Petri dish with blood sample to be viewed under a microscope.

©Carole Marsh / Carole Marsh's Curriculum Lab

Viruses are Very Virulent*

powerful!

> **genetic:** related to our DNA
> **protein:** a substance that coats genetic matter
> **antigens:** produce antibodies
> **antibiotics:** medicine that can kill bacteria
> **antivirals:** medicine that can kill viruses

The word *virus* is Latin for "slimy liquid" or "poison."

Viruses are the smallest of the microbes. They can cause flu, polio, yellow fever, smallpox, and other diseases, like COVID-19.

To survive, viruses have to take over other living cells. This is what makes them so deadly—you must kill the cell they have invaded in order to kill the virus.

A virus is a strand of genetic material covered with a *protein* shell. The genetic material inside a virus lets it copy itself once it has invaded a cell. A virus may also be covered by proteins called *antigens* that help it invade healthy cells.

Our immune system recognizes a virus by its antigens. When a virus reproduces, if often changes (including its antigens.) And so, the virus may go undetected in your body. A big change in the antigens of a virus may lead to an epidemic. Why? Because so few people would have any immunity to the *new* virus. This is what happened during the 2020 COVID-19 pandemic.

The influenza (flu) virus is good at changing easily and quickly. This is why scientists have to come up with a new flu vaccine each year. They hope to match the vaccine with the new strain of flu. And that's why instead of having long-term immunity to the flu, we need to get a new vaccine each year.

Getting a disease and surviving it can produce antibodies and immunity, but not always. You may or may not have antibodies. They may go away. Immunity is not always a given. That is another reason vaccines are so important.

While we take *antibiotics* for many illnesses, they do not work against viruses. Some viral diseases do have vaccines. Scientists are working on *antivirals* (which are not as powerful as antibiotics) in hopes of preventing diseases. After COVID-19 began to infect people, scientists around the world raced to develop an effective vaccine for this deadly disease.

©Carole Marsh / Carole Marsh's Curriculum Lab

Where Do Germs Come From?

reservoir: a person, plant, animal, or other host where germs can live and grow, but they do not affect the host

Germs live everywhere! You can find germs (microbes) in:
- the air
- on food, plants, and animals
- in soil and water
- on almost any surface
- on your body

Many infectious diseases live in animal hosts. These animals act as a *reservoir* of infection.

Germs that live on or in animals can infect other animals through:
- bites
- contaminated food, soil, or water
- fleas, ticks, flies, mosquitoes, or lice that bite the animal

When an infected flea, tick, fly, mosquito, or louse bite humans, they can transmit the animal disease to them. Fortunately, most animal germs do not adapt well to living in humans.

Just a few diseases a human can get from an infected animal include:
- anthrax
- cat-scratch disease
- hantavirus
- plague
- rabies
- tularemia
- malaria

An example of a "reservoir" may be a bat or a monkey that has infectious microbes living and growing in them, but they do not get sick. When these microbes "jump" from one animal to the other, or in some instances, from the host to a person—that's when the disease "breaks out."

Just hanging around.

©Carole Marsh / Carole Marsh's Curriculum Lab

Are Germs Coming for Us?

> **zoonotic:** *(pronounced ZOO NOT ICK) diseases that can be transmitted from animals, birds, or insects to humans; also called zoonoses (pronounced ZOO NO SIS)*

Sometimes, it seems like germs are escaping from their environment into ours. They are! Most of the time, diseases can live in animals with little harm. However, when a habitat is disturbed or destroyed, microbes can move from their animal host to humans, who have no immunity to the diseases these germs can cause.

What kinds of events can create this animal-to-human transmission?
- Forest destruction: when rainforests are chopped down to create farmland.
- Pollution: when untreated human waste pours into waters that may be used for drinking or bathing.
- Breeding grounds: when stagnant water is left for mosquitoes to breed and carry diseases such as malaria to humans.
- Overcrowded populations: where diseased animals may live too close to humans.
- Worldwide travel: which can bring a disease from one part of the world to another very quickly.

In an Ebola outbreak, doctors often track human infection and death back to monkeys infected with the disease.

As we suspected with COVID-19, a disease infection from a bat to food consumed by humans that is then transmissible to other humans, can wreak havoc around the planet. Here are just a few examples of zoonotic diseases. Six out of 10 diseases humans get are from zoonoses.

Mad Cow disease: The human version is believed to be caused by eating beef from diseased cattle.

Avian flu: A disease caused by infection from certain viruses in birds. They can then go on to infect other birds and animals. Such bird flu viruses have been known to infect humans.

Lyme *(pronounced LIME)* **disease:** The disease is transmitted via an infected deer tick.

Cat-scratch fever: Comes from infected fleas on cats.

Rabies: A disease spread through the bite of an animal like a dog, raccoon, fox, bat, or skunk.

A few others include: West Nile virus; plague; brucellosis; and emerging coronaviruses such as COVID-19.

In summary, germs may stay hidden or dormant, often not even making their bird or animal hosts ill. But under certain circumstances, such diseases can "jump" or "spillover" to human populations.

©Carole Marsh / Carole Marsh's Curriculum Lab

Living with Germs Successfully: YOU CAN DO IT!

DNA: *deoxyribonucleic acid; a long molecule that contains instructions for making all the proteins in our bodies.*

Since we're stuck with germs—good and bad—we need to learn to live with them.

Once upon a time, when people did not know what germs were, they were stumped how to help themselves. It is perhaps surprising how very long ago people did at least start to figure out how to avoid germs or react during an outbreak. We may think quarantining, wearing masks, and social distancing are new in defending ourselves against germs, but they are not.

Today, we know that protecting ourselves against bad microbes is the best idea. We have a lot of tools that people of the past did not have:

- We can see germs! Well, scientists could after the invention of the microscope. The ability to identify different microbes was a big help in understanding diseases and what to do about them.

- We have *immunizations* that help us avoid getting certain diseases. The discovery that vaccines could prevent a disease changed everything. Some diseases could eventually even be eradicated.

- We know much more about the essential use of good *hygiene* to ward off disease. Even basic things such as washing your hands is crucial to staying healthy.

- And, we have help from our own bodies—our *immune system*. We have learned that a healthy diet and exercise help our immune system be strong and better able to fight a disease if we get one.

- We have *research*. Today, we know much more about genetics and DNA. Scientists are even working on how to create germs that can fight other germs in our bodies!

At this time, having experienced the global pandemic of COVID-19, we are much more aware of the role that all these things play in staying well. When we find ourselves at war with germs, we understand that we need all the tools in our toolbox to fight this war. We need to be proactive and take good care of our health ahead of any possible epidemic.

You could say that germs don't respect us. They just do what germs do; it's not personal! But we sure need to respect germs, both the good and bad ones, and stay vigilant, knowledgeable, and as healthy as we can all the time, no matter what age we are.

With good leadership, great science, and the help of germ-fighters such as the CDC, WHO, our doctors and nurses, and others, the war against germs is one we can hope to win!

Your Amazing Immune System

The *immune system* is made up of the *lymph system* and *glands*, such as the *thymus*.

The lymph system is a series of channels running through the body. *Lymph*, a colorless liquid from the bloodstream, runs through these channels.

Lymph contains *white cells*, such as T-cells and B-cells.
The thymus controls the production of white cells from our bone marrow.
White blood cells fight infection.

Lymph nodes are made of dense lymph tissue that contains clusters of white cells.
These nodes filter lymph as it circulates through the body.

Ready to Rumble!

The immune system fights infection through an effective cycle of white cells destroying bacteria or viruses. The white cells produce *antibodies* against the *antigens* carried on the germs. An antigen is a substance that can help produce antibodies, but can also combine with them.

If you have been vaccinated against a disease, your immune system remembers those antibodies and destroys those kinds of germs if they try to invade your body in the future. This is why vaccines are so important. And, why you say you are "immune" to some diseases.

There are *autoimmune* diseases that can make your immune system less able to fight germs.

Calling all T & B Cells

You have *red* blood cells and *white* blood cells. If you get sick, who ya gonna call?

I Claim Immunity!

eradicated: when a disease is deemed to have been completely destroyed around the world

As you can see, being "immune" to any disease is a good thing.

Diseases killed a lot of people before two things happened:
1. The invention of the microscope.
2. The creation of vaccines.

It was a long road to the discovery and perfection of the tools to fight epidemics. Many types of things were tried. At first, only bacteria could be seen through early microscopes. With more powerful microscopes, the tiny viruses were first seen.

Although other types of disease preventions and cures were tried, the important discovery was that if you "infected" a person with a very weak form of a disease, the immune system learned to recognize the pathogen and fight off the disease if it came your way.

As we know, there was a rush to create a COVID-19 vaccine. Many other deadly diseases need vaccines or cures as well.

Since we see that epidemics can break out anywhere and possibly spread around the world, global immunization programs are key to preventing outbreaks. Over time, with successful programs, there is the possibility to eliminate a disease. One strategy is to start with children. That's why we get our "shots" and our "boosters"—so that we will not get infected and not infect others. However, to eradicate a disease completely, even people in the remotest parts of the world must be inoculated.

To show just how powerful germs are, even today, a disease such as measles can have an outbreak in a remote village where no inoculations have been done. Since people have NO immunity, the death toll for a "preventable" disease can be quite high.

Many people donate money to groups that conduct immunizations around the world in hopes of stopping a disease in full and forever.

It is always a celebration, and a big relief, when a deadly disease is deemed *eradicated*. Even then, small amounts of the pathogen that causes the disease is saved in case an outbreak erupts in the future and more vaccine needs to be manufactured. Such germs are saved in safe repositories such as the CDC.

The CDC, the Place for Germs to Be!

The CDC—Centers for Disease Control and Prevention—is headquartered in Atlanta, Georgia. This is the agency that monitors, detects, and investigates health problems of all types, including deadly contagious diseases. The CDC is made up of 12 institutes, offices, or laboratories, divided according to their particular focus. These "centers" can respond to a health crisis individually or jointly.

During the COVID-19 pandemic, the CDC has been at the forefront of information, statistics, data, advice, and more. Almost every day, we see or hear from a CDC doctor or representative on important issues, such as safety, numbers of infections, numbers of deaths, spread across the United States and around the world, and the status of the search for a vaccine.

The CDC employs almost 7,000 people in Atlanta, as well as another 2,000 around the nation. When there is an outbreak of a deadly disease anywhere in the world, the CDC is often the first on the scene and the last to leave. Like our doctors and nurses in hospitals and clinics, CDC doctors and nurses also risk their lives treating the sick. CDC workers have to be detectives, since some diseases are new and the pathogen that causes them must be found.

During the COVID-19 pandemic, CDC workers have been especially busy. Like EMS, doctors, nurses, and others, they often work in "hot zones"—places filled with a lot of infected people. Yes, sometimes, they contract the disease, get sick, and even die.

In addition, the CDC works on ALL health issues in America. Some of these are cancer, heart disease, birth defects, and other medical concerns. They also work to prevent death and disease from other public health problems. Today they focus on mental health, obesity, suicide prevention, no-smoking campaigns, the role of guns in homicides, drug addiction, and deaths from traffic accidents.

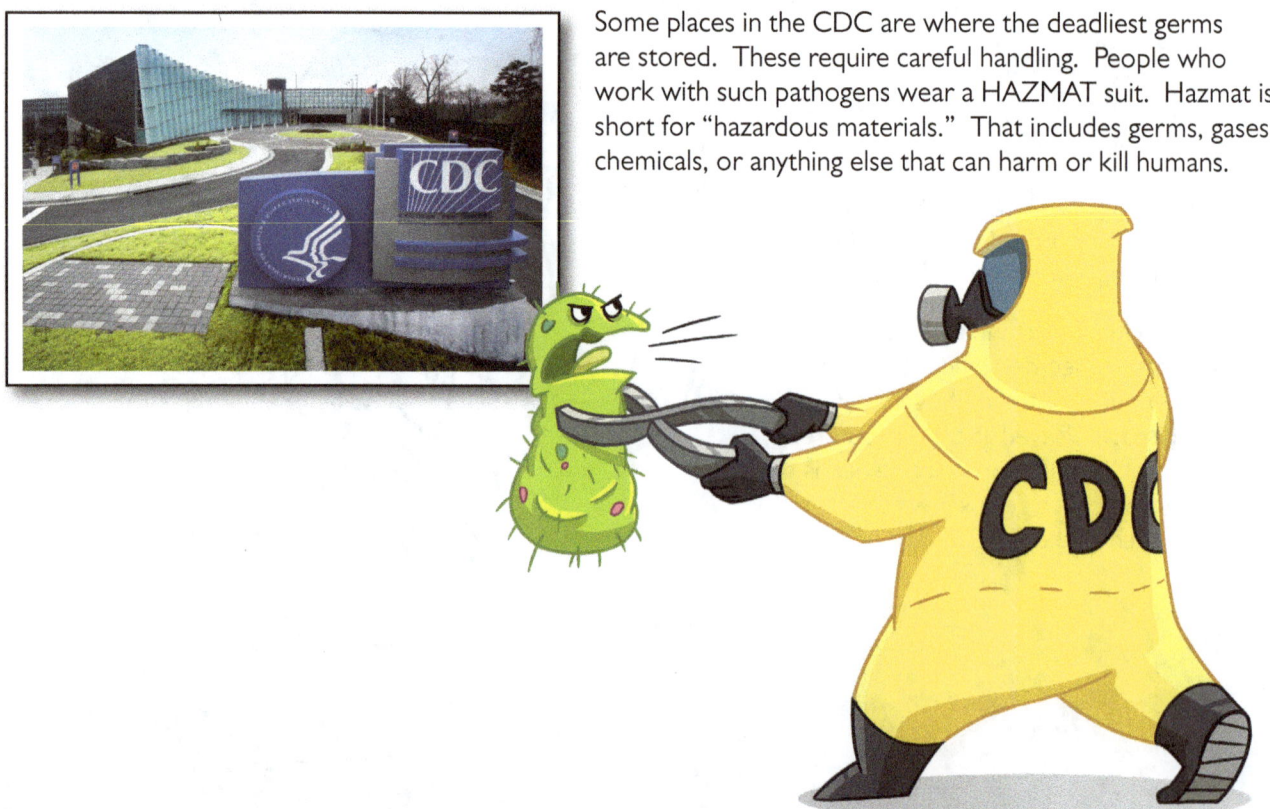

Some places in the CDC are where the deadliest germs are stored. These require careful handling. People who work with such pathogens wear a HAZMAT suit. Hazmat is short for "hazardous materials." That includes germs, gases, chemicals, or anything else that can harm or kill humans.

Genetics & the Human Genome Project

genome: all the genes that make up our DNA, the hereditary material in all living cells

As scientists continue to look for new ways to prevent and respond to disease, they believe new answers will come from genetics.

The cells of every living thing (including germs) contain genetic information.
Researchers study genetic material in bacteria and viruses to learn how they attack the body, why, and how they can become resistant to drugs that once killed them.

The Human Genome Project

The Human Genome Project was a complex 13-year program to map the entire human genome. Scientists from around the world worked to "sequence" the DNA of every human gene.

You could describe the genome as the blueprint for how a human is created.
The more we learn about our genes, their functions, roles, how they work, what can go wrong with them, and much more, the more it may help us in disease avoidance and control.

DID YOU KNOW?: THE GENES IN EACH PERSON ON EARTH ARE 99.9 PERCENT IDENTICAL!

Because of the Human Genome Project, we now know the number, location, size and order of our genes. This knowledge has let scientists screen people for genetic differences to look for who might have a genetic disease and who might be a carrier of a genetic disease.

What does the human genome look like?
Genomes are made of DNA. This very large molecule looks like a long, twisted ladder, called a "double helix." You "read" the DNA like a code. The code is made up of four chemical building blocks: *adenine*, *thymine*, *cytosine*, and *guanine*. These are abbreviated A, T, C and G.

The human genome is the complete set of nucleic acid sequences for humans. This information is encoded as DNA within the 23 chromosome pairs in cell nuclei, and in a smaller DNA molecule.

Just so you know:
- ➡ Every person has two copies of each gene, one inherited from each parent.
- ➡ Most genes are the same in every person.
- ➡ A small number of genes (less than 1 percent) are different between people.

©Carole Marsh / Carole Marsh's Curriculum Lab

WHO?

WHO Headquarters, Geneva, Switzerland

WHO is the World Health Organization. It is an agency of the United Nations based in New York City. WHO headquarters are in Geneva, Switzerland. It has six regional offices and 150 field offices around the world. WHO has 194 member nations.

WHO's primary role is to direct international health within the United Nations' system and to lead partners in a response to any global health crisis.

During the COVID-19 pandemic, WHO focused on trying to determine exactly where the outbreak started and the original source of the disease. It offers nations timely information and statistics, advice on safety measures, the timeline on a possible vaccine, and much more.

WHO also sets international health guidelines, advocates for universal healthcare, monitors public health risks, and coordinates response to global health emergencies.

WHO has played a leading role in some public health achievements, such as the eradication of smallpox, the development of an Ebola vaccine, and the near-eradication of polio.

WHO hosts World Health Day each year and publishes a World Health Report. The World Health Assembly meets annually. WHO also promotes research and provides education and information on almost every imaginable kind of health issue that affects humans.

WHO has 7,000 employees around the world and a host of Goodwill Ambassadors to help explain its programs and promote good health globally.

As you might imagine, WHO is sometimes involved in controversies when different member nations disagree on certain health policies.

No matter what, WHO's work will never end. When it comes to germs, there is always something new under the sun to tackle, and hopefully tame. A good thing that WHO is working on is reducing infant and mother deaths. A current problem WHO has tackled is bio-warfare (also called bio-terrorism) which is the use of germs, chemicals, or other toxic agents to hurt or kill people.

While it's good to know that groups such as the CDC, WHO, and others are working on global health, we can do our part by practicing good nutrition, hygiene, exercise, and getting our immunizations in a timely manner.

©Carole Marsh / Carole Marsh's Curriculum Lab

PART THREE
I'm Sick! Now What?

Most of us get sick sometimes. It might be a cold or the flu. Most of us feel perfectly awful, but we go to the doctor, possibly get medications, rest, drink a lot of fluids, maybe eat some ice cream, and soon feel better.

In past disease epidemics, this was not always so. Some diseases were especially hard on children. Polio is an example, since it struck even very young children, and was a very devastating disease. You can tell that by its official name: *infantile paralysis*.

Today, we are still plagued by illnesses such as pneumonia, HIV/AIDS, diarrhea (in some countries, this kills millions of children each year), meningitis (which can infect college ages, especially), and even measles.

It has been fortunate to see that COVID-19 has not been as hard on children as it has been on adults, especially older adults.

How you get sick, why you get sick, and just how sick you get are often affected by many things, such as:

- ➡ If you have good health and no underlying poor health conditions.
- ➡ If you live in a developed nation with good health care or in an undeveloped country with poor health care.
- ➡ If you use prevention such as washing your hands before you eat and after you go to the bathroom.
- ➡ If you get regular check-ups.
- ➡ If you are able to get all your immunizations on time and in full.
- ➡ If your symptoms are quickly recognized and you get to a doctor.
- ➡ If you get a correct diagnosis and proper treatment.
- ➡ If you follow the doctor's orders and stay home until you get well.

Let's look at a not uncommon example—the common cold!

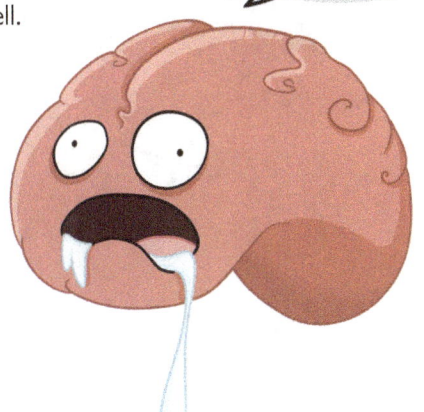

But MOMMMMM... I don't want to go to school!

©Carole Marsh / Carole Marsh's Curriculum Lab

AHHHHCHOOOO!

You go to school. One minute you feel fine and the next…
Ugh! Why do you have the sniffles, feel warm, are coughing, your nose is running, and your throat hurts?

You have a cold! The common cold. No fair! No fun!
But dangerous? *Maybe, maybe not.*

There are more than 100 different types of organisms that cause a cold. Most of them are viruses. After viruses attack cells, the infected cells release materials that cause your cold symptoms. Your immune system may kick into gear and cure your viral infection. But sometimes, your weakened health can let bacteria invade and cause other symptoms of illness. *Bah, humbug!*

Bacterial colds can be treated with rest, medications like cough syrup, and fluids.
A viral cold has no cure. You just have to let it run its course and wear off.

Your cold may even be caused by a coronavirus! *Oops.* It's ok. There are many kinds of coronaviruses, most of which cause mild to moderate upper-respiratory illnesses, like, yep, the common cold.

If you visit a doctor, they will do an exam, including take your temperature, look down your throat, into your ears, and listen to your heart and lungs. If you need a blood test, you may get your finger pricked with a needle and some of your blood put into a small tube to be tested.

> **Check with your parents and find out what the blood types are of your family members.**

What are they looking for? Antibodies. This helps the doctor see which kind of virus has infected you and just how to treat it.

©Carole Marsh / Carole Marsh's Curriculum Lab

Antibodies & Antibiotics

Antibodies are the parts of a virus or bacterium in your body that recognize the same microbes when they try to attack your body. If you have the antibodies of a disease, you are immune to it. You can get immunity by having the disease or by having gotten a vaccine against the disease.

Antibiotics are chemicals produced by one germ that kills another germ by destroying it or preventing it from growing.

Antibiotics can occur naturally in nature. Some natural antibiotics can kill a person while killing the germs that infect them!

Antibiotics are also created in laboratories. Once tested and proven to be safe, they are produced by drug companies to be sold to doctors and hospitals.

Penicillin was the first antibiotic developed in the laboratory. It was discovered—by accident—in 1940.

> **FACT-ERIA!**
> Most people carry leprosy antibodies because we have been exposed to the bacterium at some time during our lives!

Antibiotic Advice:

- It is important not to take antibiotics for a disease that it will not work against.
- If you do get a prescription for an antibiotic, be sure to take ALL your pills—even after you feel better, or the germs will flare up again and you will be sicker than ever.

©Carole Marsh / Carole Marsh's Curriculum Lab

Therapeutic Thoughts

When a new disease comes along, doctors work to discover a quick diagnosis so patients can be treated. But when a disease has never been seen before, it is a struggle to figure out what the best treatments are. This was true with COVID-19—and urgent—since the disease can be so deadly.

While some infected people had no symptoms (were *asymptomatic*), others were sick but isolated themselves and got well on their own. However, a lot of patients, especially the elderly or those who had some other illness, would often suddenly need to be put on a ventilator, into a coma, or both. Many could not overcome the infection and died. Others recovered, some spending weeks and months in the hospital. Many had long-term effects from the disease.

Over time, doctors discovered that:
- Steroids could help patients stay off a ventilator and lower their risk of death.
- A medication called *remdesivir* helped some patients.
- Plasma donated by COVID-19 survivors gave patients antibodies to help them fight the virus.
- Laying on their stomach helped some patients breathe better.

While some therapeutics worked, others did not. A medication called *hydroxychloroquine* was found to be ineffective and perhaps harmful.

The physician's code is "First do no Harm." But in an emergency, such as a pandemic, that doctors around the world work to help everyone learn what works and does not work as fast as possible is a good way to "Do Good."

therapeutic: *relating to the healing of disease*

therapeutic = pronounced **THERE A PEW TICK**

©Carole Marsh / Carole Marsh's Curriculum Lab

Pets, Pregnancy, Other Populations, & COVID-19

What? Yep, doctors have to worry about a lot of things and people (and pets!) when a new disease comes along.

As you may have heard, some groups of people have more of a problem with COVID-19 for different reasons. Physicians have to take into account all these variations.

- African Americans and Hispanics/Latinos have higher incidents of infection.
- The elderly and those with underlying conditions have a greater chance of death from COVID.
- Pregnant women and their newborn babies have special concerns related to COVID.
- We are still trying to figure out how kids (of various ages) respond to COVID.
- And then, we were surprised to find out pets can test positive for COVID.

If your pet tests positive for COVID-19, here is the current medical advice:

- Isolate them from other pets and all people.
- Don't use wipes, sanitizer, or other things like that on your pet.
- No pets have died of COVID; most recover at home with no symptoms or mild symptoms.
- Your pet should be checked by a vet before they are allowed to be around people and pets again.
- It is not believed that pets can pass the disease on to humans.
- Wash your hands after you care for your pet; wash their bowls and blankets.
- And, no, pets do not need to wear a mask, but they need to social distance—really!

The real point of this page is to show that it is important to remember a disease, especially a new one, has lots of considerations for the medical community, the general public, and us at home.

Now go pet your dog!

©Carole Marsh / Carole Marsh's Curriculum Lab

Even Kids Helped Us Get a Vaccine!

We should have seen this coming. After all, children (even as young as age 3) have participated in past vaccine trials. And in October 2020, tweens and teens volunteered to be part of COVID-19 vaccine trials!

Many of the trials have already immunized thousands of adults and gone through all the required stages to prove that the proposed vaccine is effective and safe. However, the concept is that every age will need the approved vaccine so that we have maximum immunity to the disease.

While a lot of kids might balk at being asked to get stuck with a needle, many were eager to participate, proud that they did, and hopeful that their participation would help prove that children as well as adults will benefit from the final vaccine.

One seventh grader said, "I think [what I did] could really benefit the world, and I think it would also help scientists know more about the coronavirus."

I guess you could say that you are never too young to be a hero?!

PART FOUR
Examples of Outbreaks, Epidemics, & Pandemics

The interesting thing about germs is that they are:

A. Predictable

B. Unpredictable

Outbreaks of a disease are not uncommon.
Epidemics of a disease are not uncommon.
And in the course of history, not only are pandemics not uncommon, they can come in waves and even last for years.

Although each outbreak, epidemic, and pandemic have similarities, it is also true that each of these deadly events can be so different.

➡ *Some affect a few people; others kill millions.*

➡ *Even though we can always be on the lookout for such an event, it almost always takes us by surprise.*

➡ *If we know what to do (from what we have learned from past experience), we still almost always are way too slow to react, communicate, explain, and cooperate.*

➡ *Germs mutate, so what we think we have figured out can adapt and change and the old microbe now be a new microbe to challenge us.*

The next page I write is very hard to read. It may show human nature. But what it also shows is that people can also make the same mistakes over and over even today in the 21st century.

However, the page after that describes how individual people can make all the difference in an outbreak, epidemic, or pandemic. That is good to know, learn, and not forget!

In Part Four, we will meet some germ heroes and learn how we can become one ourselves!

©Carole Marsh / Carole Marsh's Curriculum Lab

Ebola Outbreak, 2014-2016

> *index case; patient zero:* the first known infected person in an outbreak
>
> *vector:* the source of a germ, such as fleas on a rat

The Western African Ebola virus outbreak was the most widespread Ebola outbreak in history. The first cases in the outbreak were recorded in the nations of Guinea, Liberia, and Sierra Leone. There were also early minor outbreaks in other locations, including Nigeria and Mali.

A young boy was thought to be the index case in this outbreak. He died in December 2013. It was believed that the boy contracted the disease from infected bats. His mother, sister, and grandmother soon became ill and also died.

By March 2014, more outbreaks were reported in neighboring countries. Over the next months, cases grew in even more countries. The disease was spreading and infections and deaths grew. At the peak of the epidemic, more than 25,000 people had been infected and more than 10,000 died. This was a death rate of about 40%. A number of medical workers were also infected and died. Isolated cases occurred in the United States, Spain, Italy, and the United Kingdom. The epidemic was declared to be over by June 2016. Later in the year, a vaccine was developed.

This outbreak caused many problems. Many children were left orphans. The economy in some areas was greatly disrupted. Those who survived the disease often required medical care for many years. And it was believed that the virus could "hide" in a person and erupt again at some time in the future, possibly fueling a new outbreak.

Just like "Monday morning quarterbacking" after a football game, all outbreaks are later reviewed to see what was done right or wrong and needed to be done better next time. Let's look at these for each of our outbreak examples. For this Ebola epidemic:

- *WHO was criticized for delaying to take emergency action.*
- *Extreme poverty and poor healthcare contributed to deaths.*
- *Dysfunctional health care systems meant hospitals were soon overwhelmed and even closed down, causing more deaths from non-Ebola patients who could not be treated.*
- *Distrust of the government.*
- *The custom of washing dead bodies by hand helped spread the disease.*
- *The lack of containing the disease in rural villages led to the spread of Ebola into densely populated cities.*
- *Outbreaks of war in certain areas forced some international healthcare groups to have to move their doctors out of areas where they were working.*
- *The lack of trust in scientific facts about Ebola, and the lack of education about Ebola.*
- *People breaking certain rules that meant they even had to be quarantined in prisons to keep them from spreading infection.*

Spanish Influenza Pandemic, 1917-1918

This extremely deadly disease was caused by the H1N1 influenza A virus. More than 500 million people worldwide were infected (1/3 of the world's population at the time.) Between 17 and 50 million people died, making this pandemic one of the deadliest in history.

The first cases were noted in the United States, France, Germany, and the United Kingdom. Because the king of Spain was ill, the flu was called The Spanish Flu. (Actually, it was never determined exactly where the epidemic started.)

This flu came in four deadly "waves." On March 4, 1918, an army cook at Camp Funston in Kansas, in the midwestern United States, got sick. Within a few days, 522 men in the camp were ill. Because World War I was underway and troops were on the move, the disease quickly spread around the world.

A more deadly wave began in August. As more soldiers spread across America and around the world, everything from rivers to railroads and seaports to oceans carried the epidemic into every corner of the world. In this wave, younger and healthier people died.

A third wave traveled from other nations back around to the United States. And a fourth minor wave included cases in many new countries.

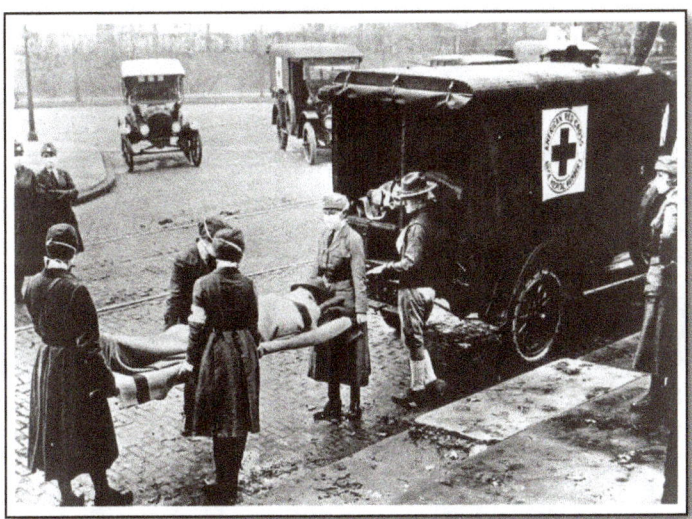

Red Cross volunteers help during the Spanish flu pandemic.

War was a major factor in the spread and severity of disease. Crowded barracks, ships, and troop trains helped the infection jump rapidly from person to person. Increased travel sped the outbreak into a full-blown global pandemic. Because soldiers were malnourished and exhausted from the stress of war and travel, their immune systems were not as strong as usual. And, "sick or not" they kept moving, taking the disease everywhere they went.

Like Ebola, later, doctors and scientists complained that these errors made things worse:

- *Medical mismanagement due to misdiagnosis. The virus was too small to be seen under the microscopes of that time.*
- *A delayed response to warn people of the outbreak.*
- *Continued mass gatherings, including a big parade in Philadelphia, Pennsylvania.*
- *A lack of masks or the wearing of them.*
- *At this time, there were no antiviral drugs and no antibiotics.*
- *Censorship of news about the pandemic in order to prevent panic.*
- *False beliefs that the disease was caused by things other than a virus.*
- *The outbreak being fairly quickly forgotten, along with the lessons learned.*

©Carole Marsh / Carole Marsh's Curriculum Lab

HIV & AIDS

The first cases of what would later become known as AIDS were reported in the United States in June of 1981. Today there are more than 1.1 million people living with HIV in the U.S., almost 38 million worldwide. More than 700,000 have died since the beginning of this epidemic.

> **AIDS:** Autoimmune Deficiency Syndrome
> **HIV:** Human Immunodeficiency Virus
> **ART:** Antiretroviral Therapy

When AIDS first came to be known, it was especially concerning because teens and young adults were at risk of this primarily sexually-transmitted disease. AIDS may have first appeared in the United States as early as 1960, but it was not until 1981 when doctors began to notice outbreaks in homosexual (gay) men in California and New York City. As men began to die of the disease, there was real fear, suspicion, and prejudice against those who might be infected.

Over time, much more was learned about this disease. While there still is no cure, there are antiretroviral drugs to help keep people well. Even more importantly, educational campaigns and materials have helped people learn more about all kinds of sexually-transmitted diseases and how to avoid contracting one.

We've come a long way from the days when people were truly terrified of AIDS, did not understand it, where it came from, how you got it, and how to avoid it. Today, if you are lucky, you will hear about such things as a normal part of a sex education class. Sex is just another subject to learn about, after all. And a disease is always something good to understand.

Like other diseases, early detection is important, being tested if you have symptoms is essential, and your body is yours to take good care of. While there was once a great stigma against AIDS patients, through improved therapies and education, death rates have dropped dramatically in the U.S.

Ryan White was a courageous young boy who contracted HIV/AIDS from a blood transfusion. Unfortunately, when this was discovered, his school would not allow him to return to classes. Ryan was 13-years-old and was given six months to live. He was a middle-schooler who just wanted to "go to school." Ryan fought against the unwarranted discrimination against him. It was because of him that people began to learn what AIDS was. Ryan fought in the courts for his right to return to school. Although Ryan died just before his high school graduation, living five years longer than expected, he became a hero for bringing the face of AIDS to people who learned you need to know the whole story before you make judgments. CARE, the Ryan White Comprehensive AIDS Resources Emergency Act was passed by Congress just a few months after Ryan's death.

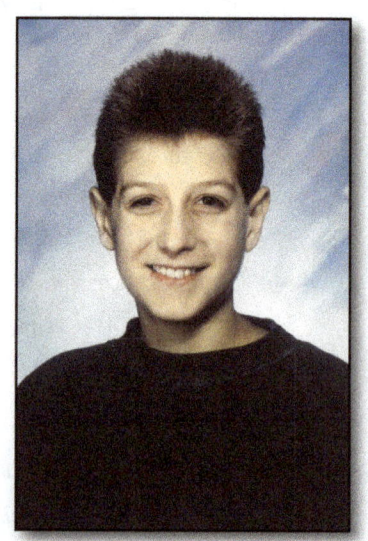

Ryan White circa 1989.
Photo by Getty Images.

COVID-19, 2020-????
Novel Coronavirus Pandemic

Off to a Bad Start

Coronavirus disease 2019 (soon referred to as COVID-19) is an infectious disease caused by *severe acute respiratory syndrome coronavirus 2 (SARS-CoV-2.)* It first appeared in Wuhan, Hubei, China, in November 2019, although there could have been prior unidentified cases. Within a short time, COVID-19 spread to other countries and around the world through person-to-person contact. Cruise ships, air flights, and other forms of international travel helped to spread the disease very rapidly. By July 2020, there had been more than 14 million cases and more than half a million deaths worldwide.

FACT-ERIA!

Masks slow the spread of COVID-19 because they help keep people who are infected from spreading respiratory droplets to others when they cough, sneeze, or talk.

America Taken by Surprise

In the United States, the disease first appeared in New York City, the state of Washington, and especially in nursing homes. Most of those who were infected were elderly, and most who died were over the age of 65 and/or had underlying health conditions. However, even those younger and healthier soon found that the disease was very hard on them. Some children died of the disease.

Pandemic, Panic, & Politics

The major problems with COVID-19 are that it is very contagious, can be spread through close contact, crowds, touching infected surfaces, and is much more dangerous than the regular flu. There is no cure and for many months, no vaccine. Primarily due to many issues, the disease spread especially rapid in New York City, but later, in almost every state. Every day was showing new record numbers of infections and deaths. With a lack of leadership from the federal government, many hospitals found themselves short of beds and essential supplies.

New York City transit bus requiring masks to be worn.

Soon there was great confusion and disagreement over what the federal government was responsible for and what states could and should do to protect citizens. All this led to a variety of "stay home" quarantine orders, disagreements over the wearing of masks, and other preventive issues like social distancing. While most people understood that handwashing and sanitizing surfaces were important, the disease continued to spread.

When there was a slight lull in new infections, some states reopened business and some people grew lax in mask-wearing. This created a surge in cases, especially from people crowding onto beaches, packed into bars, and otherwise letting down their guard. There was also a lot of confusion and disagreement over science, the cause of the disease, and many other things that did not help America deal well with this unprecedented crisis.

Learning Curve

As you will see, we had clearly not learned enough from past pandemics to be prepared for this one:

- A lack of preparedness of plans, supplies, and prevention in spite of some warnings that an epidemic could happen at any time.
- The CDC, WHO, and leaders and politicians gave conflicting reports and advice.
- A lack of information, misinformation, and disinformation made decision-making and compliance with the best preventive practices more difficult.
- Denial, disbelief, blame, and other emotional issues made matters more complex.
- Not sticking to "flattening the curve" (to prevent a rise in infectious cases) created a second surge of infections sooner than might have happened.

Heroes, Helpers...& Horrors

In spite of confusion, disagreements, and the fact that America is made up of 50 separate states—each making its own decisions—hospitals, healthcare workers, and others became virtual heroes for working hard to save lives, while risking the odds that they might become infected and take the virus home to their families. We watched with horror as ICUs (Intensive Care Units) filled with COVID-19 patients, the lack of personal protection such as masks and gowns for medical workers, the number of deaths, the expansion of hospitals onto football fields and other venues, and bodies stored in refrigerated trucks. People could not even visit their family in hospitals or hold funerals.

People in quarantine/isolation/under stay-at-home orders felt helpless, confused, angry, and wondered when things would get back to normal, if they would get sick, die, have a job to go back to, and much more. The elderly in nursing homes had a hard time since families could not visit. Even patients in the hospital who died of COVID-19 did so without family members by their side. Some healthcare workers got infected and died. Many people were put on ventilators to help them breathe; some stayed on them for a long time or were put into a coma. While some people survived, they often were still quite ill and even when they went home had a long recovery and required rehabilitation.

To Open or Close?

Because of the high contagion of the disease, many businesses, public events, sports venues, and even all U.S. schools were forced to close. This created an economic crisis. Many people lost their jobs and had to go on welfare or apply for unemployment. Students had to finish the school year via online learning. There were shortages of many essential items, including toilet paper and hand sanitizer. As transportation and manufacturing slowed, some people panicked and bought more supplies than they needed, creating even more shortages.

The U.S. government instituted a Paycheck Protection Plan which provided some people money until they could get back to work. Small businesses were also helped out. Over time, many small businesses closed for good and some large chains went bankrupt. As stores and shops were slowly allowed to reopen, we found restaurants with few tables (but you could pick-up curbside), and many new ways to try to stay in business while abiding by the rules of masks and social distancing. Even Disney World managed to re-open, while movie theaters struggled to do the same. Sports was another on-again/off-again situation when players and staff tested positive for COVID-19. Even the 2020 Olympic Games were postponed for a year.

Ongoing Problems

A big problem is that many people who are infected with COVID-19 have no symptoms (are *asymptomatic*) and can spread the disease if they do not get tested and isolate themselves. A slow start to testing, lack of testing supplies, and ongoing issues with testing made matters worse. Testing lines were long and getting the results initially took days or weeks.

Some groups were especially hard-hit by the coronavirus—the elderly, African Americans, Hispanic Americans, and those with underlying medical conditions. People who were out of work a long time feared being evicted from their homes. Food banks tried to provide for those who needed help.

Decisions regarding how to handle the start of the school year flummoxed everyone. Schools had to adapt their buildings to have students sit farther apart and perhaps only attend every other day or so. Some schools started in August; others opted to wait as long as possible. Many students started the school year the way they ended the last one: at home and online. College students often were at school just a week before the numbers testing positive forced them to return home or quarantine in their dorms. Some schools started their sports programs; others did not.

Many employees found themselves working from home. Some families worked from home *and* home-schooled!

Yes, it was sort of a zoo and pretty topsy-turvy, but the germs did not care. The pandemic continued. In spite of that, people found creative ways to cope, tried to be patient, and helped one another out as they could. Life went on, which meant a national election for president, hurricanes in the east and wildfires in the west, and an ongoing struggle with race relations in the Black Lives Matter movement..

Looking Ahead

Around the world scientists began working on a vaccine. They hoped to get any potential vaccine in trials to be tested so that they could be approved by the FDA (Food and Drug Administration.) Even then, it was unknown how long it would take to get an approved vaccine, manufacture enough vaccine to supply the world, and if people would take the vaccine when it became available.

While some people thought that having a lot of people infected with the COVID virus would eventually produce a "herd immunity" where infection rates drop, this proved not to be a good reason to ignore mask-wearing, social distancing, and other good practices.

All pandemics eventually run their course. History shows us that this can take years, that many people can die in the meantime, that many waves of the disease can occur, and that people who have had the disease might even be able to get it again. Also, people who recover from COVID-19 may have ongoing health issues.

It's a Small World, After All

If all this sounds scary, it is. We could say that kids did a good job studying at home, washing hands, and doing what adults told them to do to be safe. But, to be honest, many adults, including those who are "in charge" did not do so well in their role to protect us and keep us safe. It is good to say "we will learn from our mistakes," but it is better to know as much as you can about such a dangerous thing as a pandemic, be prepared, have a plan, and work together to make such a crisis be less disastrous.

We know what happened/is happening in America, but what did other countries do during COVID-19? Different nations did different things.

- Because some had endured epidemics, outbreaks, and pandemics of deadly diseases in the past, they were better prepared to react fast and fully to this crisis. Their leaders had a plan, implemented the plan quickly, and citizens cooperated with the plan (even all its inconveniences) because they had learned that's what it took to stop a pandemic.

- Any country that quickly closed its borders so that infected people could not enter avoided some unnecessary contagion. (The closing and opening of borders continue.)

- Every country that had plenty of essential supplies on hand and emergency plans for extra field hospitals, beds, doctors, nurses, and more, were better prepared to deal with the crisis.

- Nations who listened to scientists and other medical authorities, were better prepared to adhere to social distancing, mask wearing, good hygiene, and shutdowns as necessary to prevent as much illness and death as possible.

- Leaders who mandated masks, social distancing, no large groups, and other helpful methods had fewer cases of disease, fewer deaths, and a better chance of staying at work and school once they could return to them.

- Those areas that worked hard to "flatten the curve" with the most cooperation of its citizens eventually moved toward the lowest cases and deaths.

- Areas that "opened back up" too soon, failed to follow precautions, and allowed large groups to gather, often had a great increase of cases, hospitalizations, and deaths. It was also more difficult to get things back under control and keep them there.

herd immunity: in some epidemics, enough people finally get the disease (or a vaccine) and become immune to it. The virus dies out because it has no one left to infect.

©Carole Marsh / Carole Marsh's Curriculum Lab

As you can see, in many ways, there were a lot of mini-pandemics, you might call them. A lot depended on how fast, how fully, and how faithfully the most citizens put best practices into use. Some things were beyond control, such as weather, perhaps travel into a state by infected people, lack of or limited testing, and more. But the more a formula of doing the right things as soon as possible for as long as possible was adhered to, states, and nations fared better in the long run.

One problem was the realization and acceptance that:

1. Some infected people had no symptoms but were still contagious.
2. The incubation period was from 2-14 days, so if you had symptoms, you needed to quarantine yourself in your home away from others.
3. People who seemed perfectly healthy could be "shedding" the virus.
4. Having any underlying health issues could be dangerous no matter your age.
5. Every patient is different; children can be infected and infect others.
6. Even preventive efforts may not keep a person from being infected.
7. This new disease may change, adapt, and mutate.
8. There is probably a long time between working on a vaccine and actually getting one to every person.
9. We do not know everything about this disease and how it will progress.
10. The disease may be spread through the air (aerosolized.)
11. Family and friends can be infected.
12. This virus has no set timetable convenient to us getting back to "normal."

SPECIAL AUTHOR NOTE:
As a grandmother of middle schoolers, I want to say how proud I am of all the kids I know who have handled this pandemic so well! This is a life-changing event. It was unexpected. But you did what you had to do, were helpful to your parents and teachers, did not whine too much, and continue to amaze me with your cooperation, good spirit, ability to change and adapt, creativity, and optimism! You have endured and learned skills that will come in handy all your lives! Good job!

©Carole Marsh / Carole Marsh's Curriculum Lab

Growing Up with Vaccines!

Here is a basic chart of common immunizations and the ages they are given.
Most of the time, when you enter school, they will want a copy of your immunizations.
It's sort of a report card on your body being on time or caught up for any recommended shots.
Shots can be given by a pediatrician, your regular doctor, or are available at your local health department.
Parents will always check with a doctor to be sure you are due for your shots and that they are ok for you to take.

IMMUNIZATION	AGE	DOSES
Chickenpox vaccine	12 months	2 doses
Diphtheria, tetanus, pertussis	2 months	5 doses
Influenza vaccine	6 months	Every year
Hib vaccine	2 months	4 doses
Hepatitis A vaccine	12-23 months	2nd dose 6-18 months later
Hepatitis B vaccine	Shortly after birth	2 more doses
HPV	11-12 years old	
Measles, mumps, rubella	12 months	2nd dose at 4 years of age
Meningococcal	11 years old	2nd dose age 16
Pneumococcal	2 months	4, 6, and 12 months
Polio vaccine	2 months	4 and 6 months, 4 years
Rotavirus	2 months	4 and possibly 6 months
Serogroup B Meningococcal	16 years, per doctor	
Tetanus, diphtheria, pertussis	11 years old	

Source: CDC
(For informational purposes only; not to be used as medical advice.)

PART FIVE
LOOKING AHEAD:
How Do We Get Out of This Mess?

Even in the midst of this national and international crisis, people began to look ahead.

- 2020 was a presidential election year and there was much debate and discussion about how this would work out. Campaigning and related events took a backseat to COVID-19.

- There were disagreements over whether we were still in the First Wave of infections, the Second Wave or ??? No one really knew.

- Fortunately, many pharmaceutical companies were hard at work to create a possible vaccine, test it, and try to get it approved, manufactured, and to people around the world who desperately needed immunity against this disease with no cure.

- A lot of people grew somewhat acceptant of the "new normal" of wearing masks, working from home, online school, Zooming with friends, and worked to keep themselves and others healthy and avoid risk of infection. Others sort of threw in the towel and preferred their freedom not to wear a mask, to party in large groups, and otherwise mostly ignore the pandemic. Nothing was easy; even baseball could not quite pull off having even an "irregular" season due to infections on teams.

- The news media, social media, and pretty much everything else was still "all COVID, all the time" as things changed every day with good and bad statistics, new information, corrected myths and assumptions, and, always, ideas of what would be best and how soon could we get that shot in our arms.

- Around the world, everything was in great flux. By now, America had the highest numbers of cases and deaths. Places like China, that had passed their peak of infections, saw cases ramp back up. It was unclear if there would be repeated "waves" of COVID around the world. And no scientist thought we would reach "herd immunity" ahead of any vaccine, so that hope was pretty much dashed.

- In 2021, America began the year with some approved vaccines for health care workers. In the meantime, a post-holiday surge of infections caused hospitalization and death rates to explode. It was hoped this would eventually ebb as more vaccines were dispensed to the general population.

©Carole Marsh / Carole Marsh's Curriculum Lab

Ongoing Pandemic Issues

Testing, Testing, One, Two, Three

From the beginning, testing was a big problem. Just a few things that are still ongoing:

- not enough test sites
- not enough testing material
- slow lab work and so delayed results
- false positives; false negatives
- not enough people tested

Economic Considerations

People need to work to pay their bills. While the U.S. government offered stimulus money, and other funds to people and companies, it remains to be seen how America really will get back to work, especially with some hard-hit places having to re-close due to rampant infections.

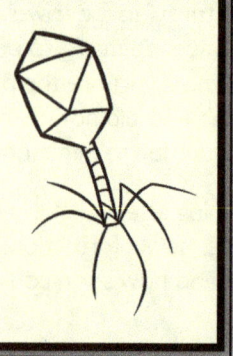

FACT-ERIA!

Even in modern times, isolated groups such as the Inuit people of Alaska have suffered from common diseases. These diseases kill off large numbers of people unless immunity is established.

Vulnerable Populations

From the beginning of COVID-19, it was clear that the elderly, those with other illnesses, poor or a lack of healthcare, in crowded conditions (such as a nursing home or a prison), and more, were at a much greater risk of contracting the disease.

The Unknown Unknowns

Until early vaccines appeared, the virus remained in charge. Even as vaccines began to be given around the world, new mutations of the COVID-19 virus surfaced. The first mutation was seen in Great Britain, again causing shutdowns. Another mutation was found in South Africa. It was hoped that enough vaccine could be produced and that enough people would get one to begin to turn the tide against this deadly disease and its new strains, often more contagious than the original virus.

COVID Quarterbacking

Although this pandemic is probably not over by the time you get this book, we have already learned many things that:

1. We wished we had known about pandemics.
2. We wished we'd done sooner or more fully.

It's important to remember that a pandemic is a bit like a hurricane. You may not know when one is coming, but you know that it will. You do not know if it will come to your area, but it may. And, that being prepared is a lot better than being unprepared, or under-prepared.

YOU are the quarterback!
Answer the following questions.

1. How far ahead should we prepare for a disaster such as a pandemic?
2. Who should be in charge of this preparation?
3. Who should know what the plan is, where the supplies are, how will we communicate?
4. What is our role in keeping up with information, advisories, and advice?
5. How does learning about past pandemics help us in current or future ones?
6. What role should federal, state, and local leadership play in a pandemic?
7. What is the role of the average citizen in a pandemic?
8. Which information sources should we trust?
9. How can looking out for ourselves help look out for others?
10. What role do EMS, healthcare workers, researchers, scientists, the CDC, and WHO play during a pandemic?
11. How is a pandemic like a natural disaster?
12. Are we "all in this together"? If so, what does that mean?
13. If YOU were in charge of the COVID-19 pandemic, what would you do differently?
14. What part can patience, cooperation, maturity, and kindness play in a pandemic?
15. What can you do instead of whine? How can imagination and creativity help?
16. What role does taking personal responsibility play in a pandemic?
17. How can you remain cheerful and optimistic in a pandemic?
18. Does anything about this pandemic inspire possible career choices for you?
19. How can you "take charge" of your own education in a pandemic?
20. How can you most help your family during this pandemic?

©Carole Marsh / Carole Marsh's Curriculum Lab

The Endgame

It was a big relief to see early vaccines approved by the FDA soon released. There was a struggle to get vaccines, especially those that had to be kept very cold, transported. There was a lot of confusion about when and where people could get a vaccine and who would go first, second, third, etc. Healthcare workers got the first vaccines, then those in nursing homes or over age 65 with underlying conditions. Soon, it seemed, vaccines would be available in more locations such as local pharmacies and even supermarkets. While scientists agreed that the best hope to end the pandemic was prompt mass immunization around the world, some people were still reluctant to get a vaccine.

Will COVID Ever End?

It is believed that like colds and the flu, coronavirus disease may be around forever. However, the COVID-19 pandemic will end. How? Because people either get the disease and recover and have immunity, or, because a vaccine is discovered and keeps people from getting the disease in the first place.

In the future, there may be periodic outbreaks of COVID, but they would be less widespread. Also, we may find, that like the flu, we need an immunization each year.

In the meantime, as we see how this pandemic pans out, we should continue to wash our hands, sanitize, wear our mask, social distance, and keep up with the latest COVID-19 news. It's also always wise to stay healthy by eating right, exercising, getting plenty of sleep, and getting all our immunizations on time.

NOW is a great time to decide to make good choices and decisions to keep yourself as healthy as possible, no matter what comes!

The Future

Pandemics generally take a typical path.
There is the index case. An outbreak. If this is not quickly stanched, an epidemic often occurs. If an epidemic gets out of hand by spreading far and wide, especially across national borders, you have a pandemic. Over time, the microbe that caused all this might go dormant, not to be seen again until the next time. Or, the microbe may mutate and spread around the world. There can be waves of increase and decrease in an area, and then future waves as the disease comes and goes. A vaccine can reduce the number of infections and deaths. The more people who are inoculated, the more successful such an immunization program is. Some things depend on the germ; some depend on humans. It's not always a "one shot" cures all. Many immunizations require multiple shots a certain time period apart. Only time can tell how the COVID-19 pandemic will pan out!

©Carole Marsh / Carole Marsh's Curriculum Lab

In the meantime, what can YOU do? Here are some ideas!

1. *Be brave and patient.* Life is full of surprises and inconveniences, scary events, and curious times. How you handle and learn from them is what is important.

2. *Respect adults.* They are the ones who have to cope with crisis. Adults aren't always prepared and don't always get it right, but they worry and work toward the best outcomes possible.

3. *Study hard.* There is a reason for school. One day you will be the adult facing the crises of your times. Whatever your job or role, what you learn today will be part of the backbone of your strength to cope with unexpected situations.

4. *People sacrifice.* It's not just policemen, soldiers, and firefighters who put their lives on the line to keep us safe. Today we see how important first responders in medicine are—doctors, nurses, EMTs, and others—as they risk their lives to save ours. Appreciate them.

5. *Character counts.* Build good character traits that will serve you well in your future role as a respected, helpful, hard-working, responsible adult. That is what you need to be when you grow up.

6. *The future is always coming.* By the time you get your education, there will be essential jobs that don't even have names yet. Study hard so you will be prepared for anything. We are counting on you. The children you have when you grow up will count on you to be up to the task of being a responsible adult.

7. *Everything is not always as it seems.* Many people did not understand why we stayed home from school and work. We did it for many reasons: to avoid illness, to slow the transmission of the disease so hospitals and caregivers would not get overwhelmed, and to protect those who are especially vulnerable to the disease, such as the elderly and those already sick. It shows our unselfish side to be Good Germ Citizens!

8. *Learning for Life.* Sometimes kids wonder why many things are important to learn about. The coronavirus epidemic is an example of the fact that we can learn how to do things better next time. And that there is ALWAYS a next time!

9. *Remember it's a small world.* We are more interconnected to people of other nations and cultures than ever. If we can work to be good citizens, then we can work as one nation and with other nations, since, as we say, "We are all in this (and everything else too, really) together."

10. Consider NOW a career where you can make a difference in the world and prepare for it. Surely you can see that WE NEED YOU!

©Carole Marsh / Carole Marsh's Curriculum Lab

The Greatest Teachable Moment Ever!

Every generation has its big "teachable moment." For some, it was a war, like World War I and World War II. For others, September 11, 2001, the day terrorists attacked America, was the Big Moment in their lives. But COVID-19 is a time that people living now, young and old, American, Chinese, Indian, or any other, will always have in common and never forget. We will probably think of it as a terrible time, especially if anyone we know had the virus or died from it. But there is so much that we can learn from hard, dramatic, unbelievable times. I'm sure that you will hear more about the COVID-19 pandemic than you want to for longer than you want to. But in the meantime, think on these things:

You survived! That's a pretty big deal. Each of us survive things over the course of our lives, but a pandemic is a pretty big thing to have lived through.

Appreciate others! Yes, a lot of folks acted bad, argued, and worse. But look at our hero healthcare workers. Look at our helpers that still picked up the trash, cleaned our teeth, treated our pets, taught us online, preached online, sang online, and more. A lot of people were very, very good. You were probably one of them.

Learn all you can! You can see that the more we knew about the history of pandemics, the more it helped. Those who had studied viruses and vaccines for years and years came to our aid. Nothing you ever learn is wasted. As you take each class, stop and think things like: "I guess I really do need to know world geography." "It is good to know how the government is actually run." "The more I learn about health, the healthier I can stay." "It's a good thing to learn about other people in all kinds of places." "Math and science are a whole lot more important than I thought." If you learn and know, then you won't have to say, "Wow, if only I had known…."

Save YOUR stories! One day, you will be the generation that remembers the Time of COVID. Your children and grandchildren (and even great-great-grandchildren) will want to know "What was it like?" They will be flabbergasted to hear you share your personal history in your own voice. They will hang over your shoulder to look at photos, newspaper clippings, anything and everything you save that means something to you. (It was never all about the adults, you know!) As a "kid" of any age, you have a unique perspective to share. Don't let it get away from you or fade. Keep a journal; make a video; draw a graphic novel [see the online Resources for more ideas] so that you have a record of "My Life during COVID-19." It will mean more to you as each year goes by.

Consider Your Future! Whatever ideas you might have had last year, you might have some new ideas about what you are interested in, what you might like to study, where you might like to work, what you might like to do, how you might make a difference. Go for it! Start now!

Be Kind! Now you know what "We're all in this together" really means. Around the world, kids have felt like you have. Some have been scared, lost parents to COVID-19, been sick themselves. Others have had to leave school, missed the Big Game, postponed vacations, missed friends. Everyone has been sad, lonely, worried, frustrated, aggravated, cranky. There might have been tears. We might have acted out. And we might have been big helps to our parents and brothers and sisters. So, as you go through life—with or without COVID—be nice, be kind. You'll never be sorry about that!

©Carole Marsh / Carole Marsh's Curriculum Lab

COVID CALENDAR RECAP

COVID CALENDAR RECAP

Let's look at an overview of COVID-19 as it transpired to see how all this worked out month-to-month and day-to-day in a real pandemic.

Have you heard of the Butterfly Effect? This is when a very small action in one place (let's say the flap of a butterfly's wings in Africa) can end up having a dramatic affect at a great distance (for example, a Category Five hurricane in Florida) on the other side of the world. That's a bit how the coronavirus disease seemed to start—just an ordinary day in a Wuhan food market.

DATELINE: Wuhan, Hubei, China, November 17, 2019
The first confirmed case of an infectious disease caused by severe acute respiratory syndrome coronavirus 2 (SARS-CoV-2) is documented.

SYMPTOMS: None; fever, cough, fatigue, shortness of breath, loss of smell or taste
DIAGNOSIS: Nasal swab test; chest CT scan
ONSET: 2-14 days from infection
SPREAD: Close contact with infected people who cough, sneeze, or talk and spread droplets of contaminated material; later we learned that droplets could be aerosolized, or spread through the air, lingering for you to pass through.
PREVENTION: Frequent handwashing, quarantine, isolation, masks, social distancing, avoid crowds
VACCINE: None
TREATMENT: Possible hospitalization, possibly being put on a ventilator or into an induced coma
COMPLICATIONS: Pneumonia, viral sepsis, respiratory disease syndrome, kidney failure, cytokine release syndrome, blood clots, multiple-organ failure
FATALITY RATE: 4%

SOURCE: Immediately there was universal concern about where this novel (new) coronavirus came from. It was believed to have been from a bat (or bats) hanging above food in an outdoor market in China. We still do not have sufficient proof of this. But once the virus escaped into a human population, the focus was on how it spread and how to stop it.

RESPONSE: The World Health Organization (WHO) worked with China on the best and most accurate testing methods. The U.S. National Institutes of Health, the U.S. Centers for Disease Control (CDC), and others went on alert to recommend ways to try to contain the epidemic since no vaccine was expected until 2021. A goal of "flattening the curve" of infections to keep a constant wave of surges down was recommended.

HEALTH CARE: In China, and as the virus began to spread, hospitals, healthcare workers, scientists and others went into action to care for patients, add beds, temporary hospitals, locate equipment and all else needed to control the eruption that was beginning to look more and more like a possible worldwide pandemic.

COMORBIDITIES: As early cases grew, deaths occurred, autopsies were performed, and data collected, it was clear that most who died of this disease were elderly and had at least one underlying negative heath issue (comorbidity.) These included asthma, pulmonary diseases, cystic fibrosis, smoking, drug use, and others. It was also unclear if you survived the disease you had antibodies and were immune to future infection, and, what, if any, long-term effects might occur at a later date, and even if you could get the virus again.

DATELINE: Wuhan, China, December 31, 2019
The Wuhan Municipal Health Commission makes the first public announcement of a "pneumonia outbreak of unknown cause." By early 2020, the number of cases was doubling every seven and a half days and the virus had spread to other provinces. On January 30, 2020, WHO declared a public health emergency of international concern. By then, the outbreak had already spread by a factor of 100-200. The next day the nation of Italy announced its first confirmed case. The virus had spread across a border.

©Carole Marsh / Carole Marsh's Curriculum Lab

DATELINE: *New York City, New York, USA, March 26, 2020*
Early in 2020, there was little talk of a pandemic in America. The assumption was that this was a disease in China. However, through travel across borders, the disease was quietly but quickly spreading. Europe was the new epicenter of the epidemic. As people continued to travel as usual, the virus spread via infected people on airplanes, cruise ships, and other modes of travel. As a primary international destination, New York City soon found itself awash in cases of this strange new disease. Soon, it had the highest number of cases in the world.

DATELINE: *February 11, 2020*
The World Health Organization officially names the now pandemic-level coronavirus COVID-19.

> ***disinformation:*** *intentionally false information which is intended to mislead, especially propaganda issued by a government organization to a rival power or the media.*

EARLY 2020: The outbreak, resulting epidemic, and full-blown worldwide pandemic put everyone everywhere in a tailspin. This would be natural. However, a lack of information, misinformation, and disinformation confused and scared the people of most nations. Some nations had strong leadership and a pre-prepared pandemic plan in place. Others scrambled to make sense of what to do and when, wasting precious time. In America, it did not help that it was a presidential election year and that instead of clear discussion and agreement, time and energy were wasted when politics seemed to take precedence over common sense and speed. There was a lot of blaming others, false claims, and conflicting information. In the meantime, early areas affected with COVID-19 (like New York City and California) had no reasonable choice except to hunker down and make quick decisions to the best of the knowledge available. It was a scary time. Leaders did not always agree on what to do. Scientists were not always listened to. No one knew exactly where to look for the best answers. There were "conspiracy theories" about who had caused the pandemic that made no good sense and, again, wasted time and effort. When the first "STAY AT HOME" orders were given to help protect people from getting or spreading COVID-19, things settled down a bit as everyone tried to cooperate and see what would happen next.

WHAT HAPPENED NEXT: *Trying to avoid a national pandemic*

- In March and April (it varied by state), most schools closed and students were sent home to learn online.
- Stay-at-Home orders meant many businesses shut down, with employees either working from home or being out of a job. "Essential" workers included those in healthcare, education, trash pick-up, grocery stores, and some others.
- Preventive measures such as wearing masks, social distancing, frequent handwashing, sanitizing, and more, created a scramble for masks, toilet paper, wipes, and more.
- Many hospitals went into overdrive to get staff, supplies, and all they would need for an assumed great influx of COVID patients into ICUs. Shortages were many.
- Some states were worse off than others. New York City saw cases and deaths rise dramatically. The state of Washington had a serious nursing home issue. And California tried to be proactive due to the state's large population.
- While it was said, "We're all in this together," there was great disagreement from the President, White House, and Congress on down to states and local communities over what were the right or wrong things to do.

In the meantime, the virus did not care…it just kept on marching along doing what viruses do—infect people.

SUMMER 2020: *Trying to keep our cool, while everything heats up*

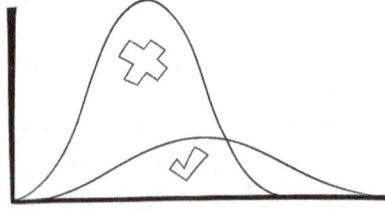

- New York City took pride in "flattening the curve," finally reducing cases and deaths, and reopening the city as slowly as possible.
- Other states became true "hot zones" of COVID-19. Florida, Texas, Arizona, California, and some other states perhaps reopened too soon or too fully, did not heed prevention recommendations, and for whatever other reasons saw a great rise in cases and deaths.
- Some state governors took things into their own hands, mandating the wearing of masks, curfews, and more. Some local mayors, who did not agree, made their own rules. Many people wanted a national law on some issues.

- In the meantime, hospitals continued to struggle with patients, treatments, and deaths, some even having to bring in refrigerated trucks to hold bodies until funeral homes could take them.

- Many places successfully opened for business by using strict methods to keep people safe. Some businesses were allowed to bring employees back under similar guidelines. It was hot and it was summer; many people went on vacation to beaches, even to Disney World when it reopened.

- To compound matters, there were protests and even riots over Black Lives Matter concerns after a number of deaths of blacks (some by police) put the problems of racism also at the forefront of our worries and considerations. There was also a major hurricane season to cope with, as well as massive wildfires in the western U.S. And, there was great concern and endless decisions to be made over whether or not kids would go back into schools, learn from home, and when and how all this would happen safely.

AUTUMN 2020: *Things improve, then the wheels fall off!*

- Schools struggle to start back virtually, in the classroom, both, neither. Things change as COVID infections ebb and flow; everyone does the best they can. One kindergartener calls her home virtual learning set-up "Poopy School!"

- The 2020 presidential election, an incredible number of enormous wildfires in the west, and a record number of hurricanes in the east dominate the news.

- In spite of strong pleas to wear masks, stay 6-12 feet apart, and not congregate in large groups, a brief lull in COVID infections begins to creep back up. Dr. Anthony Fauci warns of a dire winter of COVID/flu infections and deaths. States and citizens respond in different ways and soon there is a shocking period of record infections, hospitalizations, and deaths. Some European countries return to lockdowns and business closings.

WINTER 2020: *States try to control a bad rise in COVID, but vaccine news looks up.*

- America reaches 10 million cases, highest in the world.

- Pharmaceutical company, Pfizer, announces a 94.5% effective vaccine is ready for FDA approval. Drug company, Moderna, readies its 95% effective vaccine for approval. Others will certainly come online soon.

- President-elect Joe Biden works on plans to distribute approved vaccines as quickly as possible.

- As Americans struggle with how to handle holidays and family gatherings, mourn the deaths of almost a quarter million people to-date, they also work harder to stay safe as they await what is hoped to be vaccines for healthcare workers, the elderly, children, and everyone else beginning in December and continuing into what is hopefully a happier, healthier 2021.

2021: *America starts the new year with great concerns.*

- Political problems, frustration over vaccine distribution, skyrocketing rates of infections and death concern Americans. It appears it will take more time to get on an effective road toward ending the pandemic. In the meantime, U.S. students continued their second half of the year studies, at home or in school.

Career Opportunities Galore!

Wow! When the pandemic is over, we will look back and think, "It sure took a lot of people to get us out of this!" Think about it: Just about everyone's job changed during COVID-19. If you were a teacher, you had to learn to teach from home. News anchors had to learn to write and report and run the camera (or have their kids do it?) from home. Doctors and nurses had to learn how to treat patients long, long hours wearing more safety gear than they ever thought possible. Scientists had to learn how to work faster. Everyone had to do their jobs in a different way. Most people will be proud of how they handled such an unusual situation. Even if they were great at their jobs, many people suddenly had to be smarter, more creative, more determined. It might have even gotten a bit exciting to make good decisions fast, to change, to help, to realize all you could do when you had to. So, as you consider what you might be when you grow up, look at some of the many jobs that made the world go around better during a major worldwide pandemic! No wonder we call them our heroes! Worthy of their capes! What kind of hero do you want to be in the future?

TEACHER. DOCTOR. NURSE. AMBULANCE DRIVER. AIRLINE PILOT. PRESIDENT. GOVERNOR. BIOLOGIST. METEOROLOGIST. FULL-TIME PARENT. DAY CARE WORKER. HAZMAT SUIT DESIGNER. STATISTICIAN. VETERINARIAN. PEDIATRICIAN. VIROLOGIST. BACTERIOLOGIST. NEWS REPORTER. AUTHOR. PSYCHOLOGIST. PSYCHIATRIST. BUSINESS OWNER. ENTREPRENEUR. BANKER. SOCIAL WORKER. IMMUNOLOGIST. INFECTIOUS DISEASE SPECIALIST. EPIDEMIOLOGIST. BIOCHEMIST. BIOSTATISTICIAN. PHARMACIST. MICROBIOLOGIST. DIAGNOSTICIAN. BIOSAFETY LAB WORKER. RESEARCH ASSISTANT. LAB TECHNICIAN. MEDICAL TECHNOLOGIST. BIOINFORMATICIST. MOLECULAR BIOLOGIST. GENETICIST. VACCINOLOGIST. BIOENGINEER. RESEARCH AND DEVELOPMENT. FUNDRAISER. MEDICAL WEBSITE DEVELOPER. MEDICAL JOURNALIST. TOXICOLOGIST. ENVIRONMENTALIST. ECOLOGIST. PUBLIC HEALTH SPECIALIST. MEDICAL FIELD WORKER. INVENTOR. PATHOBIOLOGIST. HOSPITALIST. HOSPITAL ADMINISTRATOR. HEMATOLOGIST. BLOOD BANK SPECIALIST. TRANSPLANT SPECIALIST. CELL THERAPIST. INFECTION PREVENTIONIST. OCCUPATIONAL THERAPIST. PULMONOLOGIST. SPORTS MEDICINE SPECIALIST. MEDICAL WRITER. MEDICAL ILLUSTRATOR. SPACE MEDICINE SPECIALIST. HAZARDOUS MATERIALS SPECIALIST. GLOBAL MEDICINE SPECIALIST. BIOSECURITY. INTERNAL MEDICINE. QUALITY CONTROL SPECIALIST. LABORATORY MANAGER. GNOTOBIOTICIST. ANIMAL TESTING LAB SPECIALIST. ARCHAEOBIOLOGIST. INFLUENZA SPECIALIST. BIOSAFETY SPECIALIST. NURSE. MEDICAL LEGAL. NEONATOLOGIST. SEROLOGIST. CLINICAL TRIAL MANAGER. PHARMACOLOGIST. BOTANIST. ANIMAL SCIENTIST. ANTIBODY DISCOVERER. VACCINE RESPONSE EVALUATOR. EMERGING INFECTIOUS DISEASE SPECIALIST. FORENSIC SCIENTIST. CORONER. CONTACT TRACER. SURGEON GENERAL. PANDEMIC HEALTH RESEARCHER. PANDEMIC PLANNER. TRIAGE SPECIALIST. PANDEMIC RESPONSE TEAM MANAGER. MEDICAL CHEF. NUTRITIONIST. MEDICAL LANGUAGE TRANSLATOR. NURSING HOME HEALTH SPECIALIST. COUNSELOR.

©Carole Marsh / Carole Marsh's Curriculum Lab

Heroes & Helpers

Well, I guess we'll never think of Batman and Wonder Woman first anymore when we hear the term super hero, will we?

In spite of all the pain, suffering, and sorrow of this pandemic…. In spite of all the bad news of people fighting over politics and masks and more…. In spite of sad news of death, shootings, looting, and things like that…. In spite of our lives being disrupted…being lonesome…missing school and friends and sports and traditional holiday celebrations…once this pandemic is over what we will most remember are all the good people and all the good they did.

Nurses who left their families to go across the country and help out at a short-handed hospital.

Doctors who worked day and night to find enough hospital beds, even if they had to set them up in sports stadiums.

EMS run ragged with call after call after call for help.

911 operators taking those endless calls.

Testers who had to stick those swabs up our yucky noses.

Lab technicians rushing to get answers to desperate patients.

Scientists who knew they could get us a vaccine faster than had ever been done before…and did.

Coroners, and funeral home workers, and others who had to cope with the results of things not working out as we hoped.

Those unnamed people who cleaned up the messes to get ready for more messes.

Governors who turned into Mother Hens for their state.

Moms who became kitchen table school teachers.

Dads who worked hard to keep things together, in spite of everything.

Teachers who bravely risked school and often became the shoulder to cry on for kids who just couldn't understand what was going on.

Grandparents who smiled from windows even as their hearts were breaking.

Girls and boys who hung in there, wrote letters, made parades, helped fill food banks, and kept us smiling.

In spite of a worldwide pandemic that fell into our laps that we could not wrap our arms around…we could wrap our hearts around each other, wear our masks, do our part, and be heroes in our own small ways.

Yes, we really were all in this together. And when we are all out of this together, let's continue to be heroes, helpful, curious, wise, and grateful.—

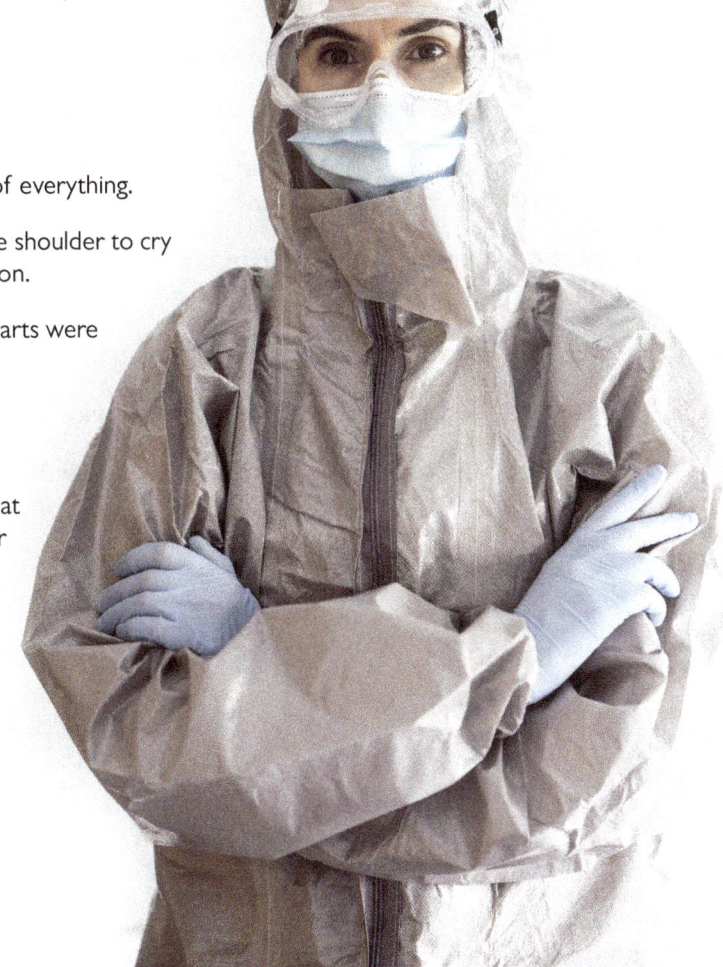

©Carole Marsh / Carole Marsh's Curriculum Lab

How You Can Help

It pretty much does not matter much what happens in the world, there is almost always a great need for help, and many ways to help. What are you waiting for? Circle the things that appeal to you that you believe you can and would do during the COVID-19 pandemic. How can you make your choices happen?

- **Write notes to people stuck in nursing homes or isolated at home.**
- **Collect money to give to people who need it because they are poor or have lost their job, or other such things.**
- **Learn about the pandemic so you can explain some things to people who misunderstand the COVID-19 disease.**
- **Collect food for a food bank.**
- **Donate to organizations that help people who need it at this time.**
- **Wear your mask when needed, wash your hands, social distance.**
- **Follow all the rules at school so there is a better chance your school does not close.**
- **Share your wifi with others who may not have access to what is needed for virtual school.**
- **Collect or share essential school supplies with kids who have none or run out.**
- **Help kids having problems with a subject via online, texting, etc.**
- **If homeschooled, help your younger brothers or sisters with subjects you have already had and understand.**
- **Build a neighborhood "little library" and stock it with books kids may need for reading or learning.**
- **Collect extra masks or gloves for those who need them.**
- **Do "thank you" notes for medical workers.**
- **Have a bike parade for someone on their birthday if they are stuck at home.**

©Carole Marsh / Carole Marsh's Curriculum Lab

But Did They Use Novacaine?

How's this for combining archaeology+technology+disease to create a cool job known as *paleogenomics*? A *paleogenomicist* studies DNA in remnants of ancient teeth using high-tech medical tools. It takes a lot of cool new jobs to get to the bottom of the question—"Did Stone Age people have pandemics?"

After a prehistoric tooth is recovered and the stuff inside it pulverized, a *molecular biologist* uses "shotgun sequencing" to extract genetic material. *Bioinformatic* specialists decrypt the data in that material and match the genetic identities to known pathogens. Archaeologists then try to figure out how this fits into some holes (uh, cavities?) in the historical record.

If you think going to the dentist is expensive, well it costs $1 million+ to crack the genetic code in a set of really (really, really) old teeth. It's like finding a needle in a haystack, or, good hits are about as rare as hen's teeth.

However, due to all this new technology and job skills, scientists have discovered hepatitis B virus 7,000 years old, parvovirus B19 6,900 years old, and evidence of salmonella 6,500 years old. Yes, all from old teeth! Scientists even believe that plague bacteria (like that of the Black Death) infected Stone Age humans 5,000 years ago.

Perhaps even more fascinating, scientists suspect that as Neolithic people gathered into larger groups (say, 10,000) and lived very close together with people and animals, they set the stage for a disease outbreak—and even a pandemic.

If you're looking for a career, maybe they need some help?
And what are they really after? The tooth, the whole tooth, and nothing but the tooth!

©Carole Marsh / Carole Marsh's Curriculum Lab

DARPA: Infectious Disease Experts on the Lookout for the *Next* Disease

Some people have interesting jobs. One of them is to be the person first on the scene of a new outbreak. Like a detective working a murder case, an infectious disease specialist has unique skills and is in a bit of a hurry to solve the question of "who dunnit?" What new microbe just emerged? How contagious is it? How does it spread? How fast? And, most of all, just how deadly is it?

Such a person might have to race around the world to be in the right place at the right time. What they see might be gross. What they do can vary on any given day or case. Time is always of the essence. They might be scared. After all, they are not immune to the mysterious, invisible microbe they are trying to track down.

DARPA, the *Pentagon's Defense Advanced Research Projects Agency*, is where you might find such specialists. They not only work on the disease outbreak at hand but also worry about future emerging unknown germs and when and where they might appear next. It is important and essential that such experts work in the background, even as we go to work and school.

By working on disease after disease, these specialists learn a lot. Disease prevention is a big deal to them. The sooner they can identify a new threat, the faster they can decipher what to do about it. No one, more than them, realizes that the world is a very small place, and that new diseases (and sometimes old ones) are always on the move. You can be sure they will be on the cutting edge of new medications, methods, prevention, and vaccine issues.

It is good to know that some people like DARPA, WHO, the CDC, and others are not only working on our behalf, but also cooperating with their counterparts in other countries to try to keep us all safe.

The least we can do is do our part: social distance; wear a mask; wash our hands; get our immunizations; and abide by other necessary rules until the "all clear" is given. Some of us might even ponder if this is a career we might live to have. Sort of the James Bond or GI Jane of germs?!

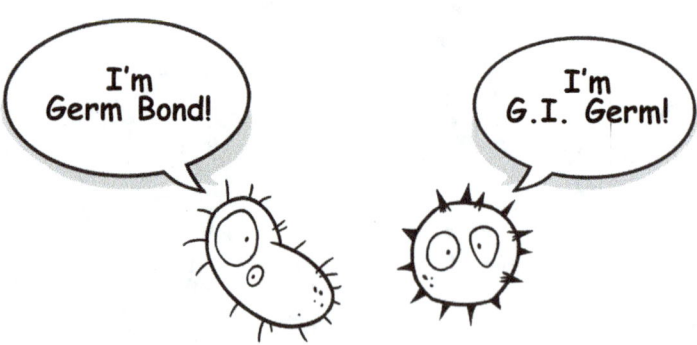

Pandemics as the Impetus to Invention!

Imagine you are a scientist, inventor, or even a tinkerer in your garage. If you saw little children who could not breathe, you might be inspired to create something to help them. If millions were dying from a disease with no cure, you might wonder, "What can I do?" Here are just a few amazing inventions brought about in this way.

IRON LUNG: During the coronavirus epidemic we learned about ventilators. An early version of a machine to help people breathe came about after a polio epidemic. This tanklike contraption was first made using out of two pumps from vacuum cleaners and a big metal box.

INCUBATOR: There was once a "pandemic" of premature babies being born and left to die because there was no way to take care of them. The first incubator, called a "baby box" held the tiny newborns and kept them warm (one of the main things they needed) until they could grow. Incubators were so unusual that the babies were shown at fairs and in circuses. An improved incubator was better able to be controlled, since one earlier version virtually "steamed" babies to death.

VACCINES: This invention came as a result of a smallpox epidemic.

INVENTIONS, GREAT AND SMALL: Not all inventions are new or big. Many are improvements of other inventions. For example, there is now a portable ventilator, a portable defibrillator to start someone's heart even on the side of the road, improved masks such as the N-95 mask, and more and better vaccines all the time.

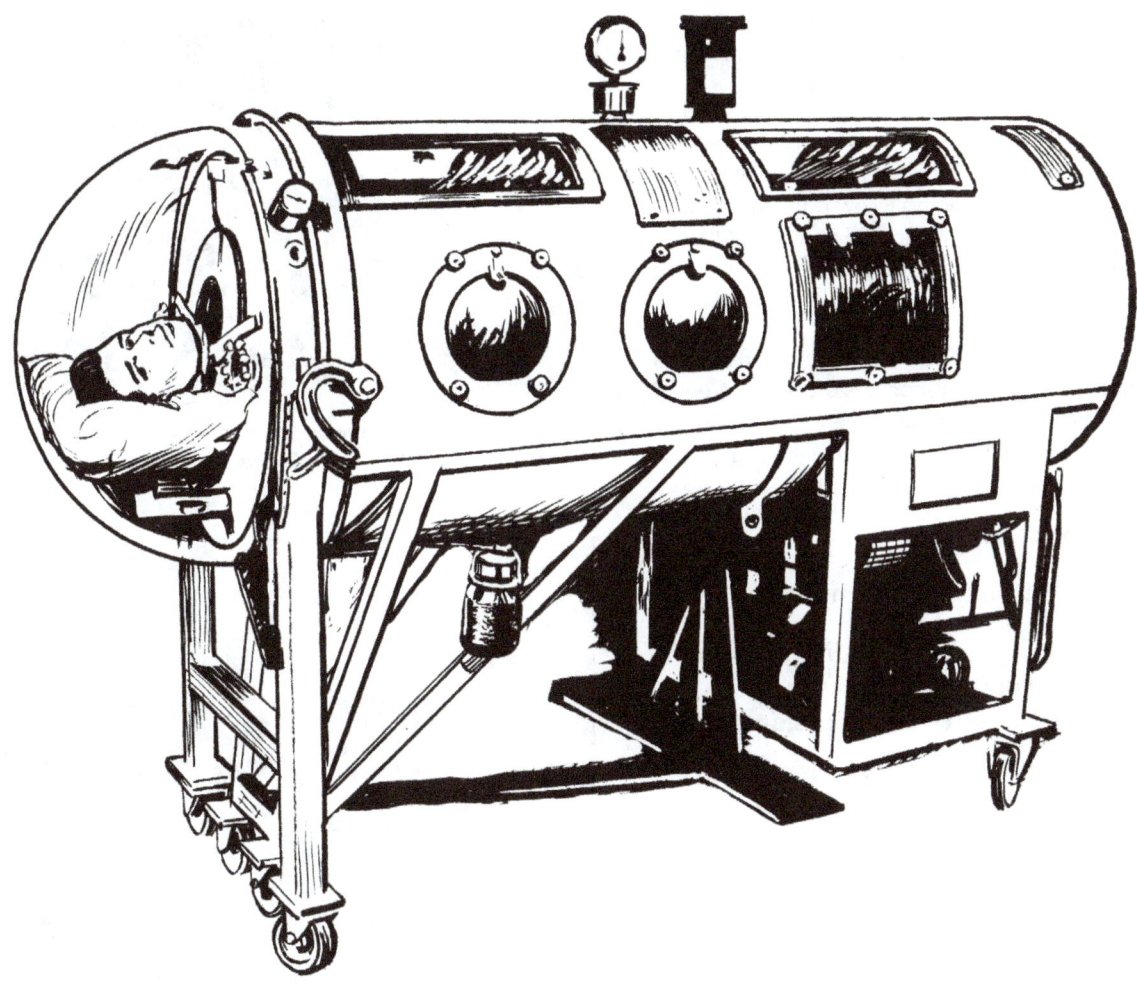

©Carole Marsh / Carole Marsh's Curriculum Lab

MORE

Heroes & Helpers Throughout History...

Balto Saves the Day!

Balto was a six-year-old Siberian Husky and sled dog. He belonged to Leonhard Seppaia.

In 1925, doctors feared that an epidemic of *diphtheria* was headed to Nome, Alaska. Young people were especially vulnerable to this deadly disease. The only serum that could prevent the outbreak was in Anchorage, Alaska, many miles away. The airplane that was supposed to bring the serum had a frozen engine and could not fly.

Desperate for a solution, the medicine was brought by train to Nenana. A musher and his sled dog team brought it to another team and that team to another team—in hopes of reaching Nome before the disease did. The world watched as the men and dogs battled a blizzard and temperatures of minus 23 degrees below freezing! They had to travel more than 600 miles over snow, ice, frozen waterways, and against high winds.

On February 2, Balto led a team into Point Safety where they expected to be relieved by the last team. When that team was not prepared to leave, Balto and his fellow dogs and musher raced the final 25 miles to Nome! They arrived at dawn. All the antitoxin ampules were intact—not a single one broken. The frozen medicine was handed over, thawed, and put into use by mid-day.

Balto had saved the day! The world cheered! Balto was a hero! Later, a statue of the famous dog was erected in Central Park in New York City. Many books have been written and movies made about this treacherous journey and super-hero dog!

Gunnar Kaasen with Balto in 1925.
(Wikimedia Commons)

Questions for Discussion:

- **Do you admire this team effort?**

- **As you journey through life, do you hope you have the creativity and courage to rise to the occasion under difficult circumstances?**

Balto and his sled team in Nome.
(myhero.com; Public Domain)

©Carole Marsh / Carole Marsh's Curriculum Lab

Buddy the Dog!

Buddy, a German Shepherd, almost age 7, was having his usual fun summer of running around and swimming with his baby puppy brother, Duke. But one day, he could not breathe well at all. Six weeks later, he was the first dog in the U.S. that tested positive for having COVID-19. It's rare, but it can happen. He probably got it from his owner. Luckily, so far there is no evidence that humans can get COVID-19 from a dog. Buddy died. Rest in Peace, Buddy! We all need a buddy at this time.

Cotton Mather

Boston, Massachusetts, USA.   1721.   Smallpox.

Time since last pandemic: 19 years

Outbreak: Boston Harbor

Symptoms: light red spots on skin that turned into bumps, filled with fluid

Response: people tried to ignore the outbreak

Cotton Mather's Background, Response, and Accomplishments:

- Studied science and medicine since childhood; overcame a teenage stammer
- Lost 2 wives and 13 of 15 children, many from infectious diseases
- Read science journals and studied Native American medicine
- Heard about a method used in Africa to stop smallpox
- Fought for the use of variolation (or inoculation) to prevent smallpox
- Figured out that tiny organisms were the cause of epidemics

Cotton Mather
https://commons.wikimedia.org/wiki/File:Cotton_Mather.jpg

Outcomes:

- Helped introduce the first vaccines made from the disease microbes
- Wrote a book of his findings, but it was 150 years before scientists believed his correct assumptions!
- Had his home bombed (it did not go off) for recommending immunizations!

Doctors Without Borders

In May 1968, a group of young doctors decided to go and help victims of war and disasters around the world. Their name in French is *Medicins Sans Frontieres*—Doctors Without Borders. Their goal was to provide aid where it was needed. They often worked in war zones in makeshift hospitals while under fire. They believed that everyone deserved medical care. It did not matter what their race, nation, gender, religion, or anything else was.

Soon, the doctors, nurses, and others were often first on the scene anywhere in the world when there was a natural disaster like an earthquake, or a war that meant there were refugees who had to leave their homes, or when there was a disease outbreak such as Ebola in Africa.

Today, Doctors Without Borders has offices in 28 countries and more than 30,000 people working around the world in many places at the same time. Just as importantly, they are an independent group. Their goal is not to play politics or favorites but to help and improve the health of those that need it when they need it.

In 1999, they were awarded the Nobel Peace Prize!

As you might imagine, Doctors Without Borders is working in America and around the world to help with the COVID-19 pandemic. Many people make donations to the group.

Dr. Anthony Fauci, The COVID Voice of Reason—Are We Listening?

For decades, Dr. Anthony Fauci (pronounced FOW CHEE) worked quietly as a respected immunologist. He is one of the world's leading experts on infectious diseases. He has also had major jobs such as the director of the National Institute of Allergy and Infectious Diseases. As a doctor with the National Institutes of Health, he served many American presidents in times of public health crises.

Dr. Anthony Fauci
National Institutes of Health

In 2020, Dr. Fauci was seen almost every day at the White House, in press conferences with President Donald Trump, and on talk shows to help explain the virus and inform citizens about all aspects of the disease. There is nothing we need more when a surprise pandemic erupts than someone who is knowledgeable, experienced, trusted, and a good communicator. Dr. Fauci is all these things.

However, his job was difficult. Some people did not want to believe all that he said. Even if they believed what he said, not everyone wanted to heed his wise advice. But Dr. Fauci had a good strategy that served him well. He stuck to his story, constantly explaining in plain English what people needed to know. The facts he shared were not ideas; they were based on science. Even when the president disagreed with Dr. Fauci, he stuck to his scientific guns and just kept telling us over and over again what was going on, what we should do about it, and what we should expect next.

If there's a fire in the stadium, we want to hear a trusted voice tell us where to go. If there is a report of a shooting at school, we want to see and hear someone we trust say, "Walk this way! Go now!" And when there is a new disease that is very contagious, we want the facts fast and things to do that really work.

Dr. Fauci practiced what he preached. He wore a mask. Once stay-at-home-orders were given, he went to his home and stayed there, broadcasting and meeting from a distance all he could. He did not just tell us what to do, he showed us how to do it. That's a great example of leadership, good communication, and faithfulness.

Even people in his neighborhood put signs in their yards thanking him. He continues to be that much-needed trusted voice in the darkness. Thanks, Dr. F.!

Edward Jenner

BACKGROUND:

- When he was 8-years-old, variolation was still so new in England that he was purged and bled first, and then got his variolation; that was not fun!
- When he became a doctor himself, he inoculated an 8-year-old boy using material from a woman who had been infected with cowpox.

RESULTS:

- This was the first vaccination! *Vacca* comes from Latin for cow.
- Some people feared that if they got a cowpox vaccine they might act like a cow, get cow diseases, or even grow horns!

OUTCOME:

- Jenner became known as the Father of Immunology.
- As vaccinations became the standard treatment, variolations were discontinued.
- While smallpox continued to kill millions of unvaccinated people around the world, it was clear that vaccinations could prevent deadly disease.

purge: to be caused to throw-up (regurgitate)
bled: to have blood drained from your body; usually with a leech!

His Was a Filthy Business!

Disease avoidance is a dirty business. That's what **John Pringle** decided in 1743.

It was in Frankfurt, Germany. The British had beaten the French in a war. More than 1,000 soldiers who had survived the war now looked like they might die from disease. Dr. John Pringle watched these men stagger into a battlefield hospital.

The men were filthy. They slept two or more to a bed. Many slept piled on the dirty floor. Soon the sick men had done what deathly ill men do. The place was quickly covered in pee, poop, vomit, sweat, and blood. Fleas and lice covered the men. The men had typhus. Most died.

Dr. Pringle was appalled. He wrote a book—*Observations on the Diseases of the Army*. His recommendations, that turned into rules and regulations, included:

- *Don't set up campsites in damp areas.*
- *Dig latrines (outdoor toilets) before soldiers are brought into camp.*
- *Keep camps well-ventilated.*
- *In hospitals, keep the patients, linens, and all spaces as clean as possible.*
- *Do not crowd soldiers into such small spaces (social distance) to help avoid disease spread.*

Pringle had the right idea. Soon deaths in army hospitals dropped by half! Other countries began to catch on and developed their ideas to keep soldiers safer from disease.

75% of Napoleon's soldiers in 1812 died not from WAR but from TYPHUS.

King Carlos IV to the Rescue!

Someone had to do it! Once a smallpox immunization was available, what good did it do unless a lot of people got it? In 1803, King Carlos IV of Spain had an audacious idea. He called it *The Royal Philanthropic Vaccine Expedition*. His goal? To get the vaccine to all parts of the Spanish Empire. There were a lot of problems to overcome—getting enough vaccine, training vaccinators, getting the vaccine where it needed to go. And where it needed to go was mostly gotten to by ship!

Carlos was one smart cookie. His plan was to set up what was really the first ever global public health initiative. It took a lot of people and a lot of planning. But perhaps the most important issue (except for getting everywhere by boat) was getting people to accept getting vaccinated. Sound familiar? Even today, when a COVID-19 vaccine seems to be near, a lot of people are already saying, "Well, I'm not gonna get it!" (Trust me, I'll be first in line!)

So Carlos had the idea to use people who spoke the many languages across his extensive empire. To use local leaders that the different communities trusted. And, to treat the patients with care and concern. Let's see how this panned out:

FIRST: It took three long, hard years to get everyone vaccinated!

SECOND: It took lots of men and ships and circuitous routes to get to all the hundreds of thousands of people vaccinated. Some devoted their lives to this cause, often losing their life to get the job done. The expeditions were full of danger; one route included trekking over land for 2,500 miles!

THIRD: How do you transport vaccine that will expire or run out and you are too far from Spain to get more anytime soon? Get creative! The first ship carried 22 orphans. Doctors vaccinated pairs of the boys every few weeks. As the first pair got some skin pustules (but not full-blown smallpox), the doctors used that to infect the next pair of boys. And so, by the time they got to their first destination they had plenty of live vaccine!

Once they got to port, the boys were adopted by local families. New orphans were gathered for the next leg of the campaign. Millions of lives (and a great deal of awful suffering) were saved through this amazing initiative! Thanks, King Carlos!

Onesimus *(pronounced OH NIS EH MUS)*

BACKGROUND: African-born slave living in Boston, Massachusetts

TIME PERIOD: 1721

EPIDEMIC: SMALLPOX

CONTRIBUTION: Onesimus told his master, Cotton Mather, about a method of preventing smallpox he had seen done successfully. In fact, he had scars from the procedure. Onesimus explained that the technique included taking a pustule from a person with smallpox and putting the puss into a healthy person through a small slit in the skin. This was called variolation. Once inoculated, the person would become immune to the disease. Like vaccinations today, someone might feel bad for a couple of days with a very mild form of the disease. But this was much better than having full-blown smallpox and possibly dying or being very disfigured (or even blinded) from the disease. Plus, the fewer people who got the disease, the slower the spread and the sooner the epidemic could be over.
Many Bostonians were petrified of this new idea and feared being vaccinated.

OUTCOME: As a slave, Onesimus got little recognition for his contribution of the idea for this new preventative treatment, even though there were other African-born Bostonians who had been inoculated successfully. Onesimus was finally able to purchase his freedom.

Vice Admiral Dr. Jerome Adams

Vice Admiral Dr. Jerome Adams is the 20th Surgeon General of the United States. Did you even know we had a Top Doc? We do, and at no time is their help needed more than during the outbreak, epidemic, or pandemic of a deadly disease.

During COVID-19, you may have seen Dr. Adams on television, advising us to follow the germwise protocols: mask up; wash up; stay apart. The surgeon general (who is over about 6,500 public health workers around the nation, has a 24/7/365 job. Although you may not see the surgeon general all the time, over the 50 years that we have had this Top Doc, you have certainly seen evidence of their work and been the beneficiary of their efforts.

If you go to the health department to get your shots, well that's part of their job. Those warnings about cancer on packages of cigarettes? That's something they did. Today they work a lot on the problems of drug and other addictions. If it affects our health, it keeps them up at night!

How would you like to have about 300 million patients? You'd probably hope they'd listen to you and heed your advice. If we know a lot more about diseases, vaccines, our school shots, good lifestyle health (like not smoking or doing drugs), avoiding obesity and more, that's due to America's public health workers—in big cities, small towns, rural areas, Native American Indian reservations, and basically anywhere we are.

During COVID-19, it has been sad to see some public health workers threatened just for helping us know what to do.

Women Germ Hunters!

It takes a village of scientists to battle germs. Men and women work hard to identify microbes, figure out what they do, and create vaccines to kill them. However, women scientists are sometimes left in the fine print and footnotes of history. Here are just a few we should thank for their fine efforts.

COLLEEN CAVANAUGH: Discovered the first chemosynthetic organism, 1980

ANGELINA ELISHEMIUS: Invented agar gel used in petri dishes to grow bacterial cultures, 1882

CAMILLE GUÉRIN: Helped develop the vaccine against tuberculosis, 1921

LADY MARY WORTLEY MONTAGU: Helped introduce the new smallpox inoculation, 1718

DR. ANNA WESSELS WILLIAMS: Developed a vaccine against diphtheria, 1894

DR. GRACE ELDERING and **DR. PEARL KENDRICK:** Developed the whooping cough vaccine, 1940

DR. MARGARET PITTMAN: Helped create vaccines against typhoid, cholera, whooping cough, and meningitis; also discovered six types of flu microbes, and helped develop the HIB vaccine 1980s-1990s

DR. ISABEL MORGAN: Helped discover a polio vaccine, 1955

DR. ANNE SZAREWSKI: Developed a vaccine to help eradicate certain types of cancer, 1990s

DR. RUTH BISHOP: Led a team that helped make a vaccine against rotavirus, 1973

DR. DEBORAH BIRX: World-renowned global health official and the White House's voice during the COVID-19 pandemic, 2020

Dr. Deborah Birx

Zabdiel Boylston, Variolator!

YEAR: 1721

EPIDEMIC: SMALLPOX OUTBREAK, Boston, Massachusetts

BACKGROUND:
- He almost died of smallpox 19 years earlier.
- Like doctors during COVID-19, he worried his work with infectious diseases could put his eight children in danger.
- He performed his first two smallpox inoculations (called variolations then) on his six-year-old son and two family slaves.

RESULTS:
- When the inoculations only brought about a very weak form of smallpox, he began to immunize his patients who wanted to protect themselves from the deadly disease.
- Many Bostonians feared that those who had been inoculated might still be contagious.
- Some other doctors questioned this new treatment; they believed smallpox was caused by bad smells or bad air, not germs.
- People who could not afford the price of variation resented people who could.

OUTCOME:
- After the epidemic ended, about half of Bostonians had come down with smallpox (6,000 people); around 15% died (844.)
- Just 2% of the people who had been inoculated against the disease got it; with improvements to the variolation, that was reduced to less than ½ percent.
- When the next smallpox outbreak hit Boston in 1792, more than 9,000 people had been inoculated and only 232 of them got the disease.

Perseverance Pays Off!

What would you do if your life's work was put-down as a dead end without value?

Almost everything was against pioneering scientist Katalin Karikó from Hungary. She left her home to come to America to do science, but her ideas were devalued and she was demoted. So what did she do? She kept right on working on what she believed in. That was messenger RNA. Her years of experiments (failures and successes) gave her the idea that this might be THE thing that could help end COVID-19. It was at a low point in her career, but not her stamina and determination, that she proved that she was right.

Using "lipid nanoparticles" (sounds cool, hey?), she figured out that this would allow a vaccine to be made that would not produce dangerous inflammation in the body. Is this a big deal? You bet! So big that Karikó and her main collaborator, Drew Weissman, will probably win a Nobel Prize! But most of us will eventually recognize her name for being someone who helped stop the pandemic and saved lots and lots of lives.

Do you ever think of giving up? Well, don't!

©Carole Marsh / Carole Marsh's Curriculum Lab

Keep Calm and Carry On

For many of us, the COVID-19 pandemic has been quite stressful.
A lot of things in life can be stressful, but you have to admit: we don't have a global pandemic every day, do we?
This is historic. What can we do to make ourselves feel less stressful?

BE GRATEFUL
At least we live in an era of smart medical thinking, good hospitals, and scientists who know how to make a vaccine. We have parents, teachers, and friends to help look out for us and keep us safe. *Try not to be anxious. Everything will be ok. Relax and do your job of being a good student and helpful to your family.*

REDUCE STRESS
Staying busy is a good way to reduce stress. Focus on the new way of doing school as an adventure. Accept change. Participate in sports or other physical activity. Take up a new hobby that helps you pass time along. Help your family and others; they may be stressed, too. *Have a "go to" stress reliever whether that's shooting hoops, reading a good book, texting your best friend, or whatever helps you feel better.*

DON'T WORRY SO MUCH
You're a kid; this pandemic thing is something for adults to take care of. They will! For every bad thing you may hear, there are hundreds of good things going on in the world. People still have birthdays, holidays, laugh, and be silly. Things will get better. *The pandemic is just part of the long story of your life.*

THE BLITZ
During World War II, families in London, England, had to put up with being bombed by German airplanes almost every night for three long years! Yes, it was a terrible thing. However, the people prepared as best they could. When sirens warned of an attack, they hurried into underground shelters until it was over. Yes, they were worried and stressed and afraid. But they were braver, patient, and helped one another. Today, the world still admires the British for their resilience and perseverance during that time. *So, Keep Calm and Carry On!*

Surprising Germ Trivia!

Viruses can replace a defective gene with a good gene ✳ Mother's milk is rich in antibodies ✳ *Necrotizing faciitis* is a flesh-eating germ that eats so fast you can almost watch it and can cause amputations if not treated immediately ✳ USAMRIID is called the "Institute," its hot zone hospital "the slammer," and its morgue "the submarine" ✳ The National Institute of Pathology warehouses a century's worth of germ samples ✳ The National Parasite Collection includes giant tapeworms that grow in whales ✳ The "Blue Suit" is a Chemturion space suit worn in biosafety level 4 labs ✳ The "Orange Suit" is a portable hazmat suit ✳ The "hatbox" and the "ice cream container" are waxed round containers used to hold biohazardous materials ✳ EnviroChem is a slime green disinfectant use to kill germs left on medical workers' clothing ✳ Lucy is the nickname for a frozen body found in Alaska that still had 1918 flu virus inside ✳ One Alaska village posted armed guards to shoot anyone who tried to enter the village and so remained Spanish Flu free ✳ Dorothy Melvin, a parasitologist, adopted "Petunia" from the pound and she became the mascot and blood donor to check for microscopic parasites ✳ Ryan White became a "hot zone" after getting a transfusion and contracting AIDS; he was also a hero for educating people you could not get AIDS just from touching someone or them breathing on you ✳ Former U.S. president Jimmy Carter was knighted by the queen for helping eradicate the guinea worm that once killed millions of people around the world ✳ Due to drug resistance more than half of pneumonia cases in the U.S are resistant to penicillin ✳ Once, college students were paid $350 each to intentionally get a cold so that scientists might find a cure—no luck ✳ E.coli is a microbe that has caused a lot of problems with things kids like, such as water parks and hamburger fast food places ✳ A common plague on the Oregon Trail was cholera; when parents got sick, kids were stuck with driving the covered wagons, hunting food, and even fighting off Indians ✳ In the pioneer era and beyond, tight quarters where disease could easily spread, especially in winter, were camps of tents and crowded steamboats ✳ Rocky Mountain spotted fever comes from a tick bite ✳ Log cabins called "soddies" were often hot zones for malaria or cholera ✳ Pioneer-era treatments for disease included onion poultices, "Indian Primp" tea, and boiled corn tucked next to the body

©Carole Marsh / Carole Marsh's Curriculum Lab

Surprising Germ Trivia! (continued)

✹ Wilma Rudolph, a there-time Olympic gold medal winner had polio as a baby ✹ Around the world, tuberculosis kills more women and girls than any other disease ✹ Astrobiology is the study of microbes on other planets ✹ Bacteria that get on your gums and teeth can travel through your body and make you sick so brush your teeth ✹ Most microbes that infectious disease specialists work on today were unknown 25 years ago ✹ Infectious diseases are the third leading cause of death worldwide ✹ Gray Zone=where the normal world and hot zones meet ✹ Abigail Adams, wife of U.S. president, John Adams, spent days scrubbing floors with hot vinegar to try to stop an epidemic of typhoid; she also "smoked" any mail, hoping to kill germs on letters and packages ✹ Savannah, Georgia's first epidemic of Yellow Fever, killed 666 people in 1820; there were so many dead bodies being carted down the cobblestone streets, thick pads were put on the horses' hooves so as not to disturb the ill inside their houses ✹ Scientists are working to create antibiotics from bat spit, giant leeches, and Komodo dragon saliva ✹ Scientists are working with a microbe that can remove heavy metal from water ✹ Bio-remediation is the use of plants and microbes to clean up pollution ✹ The Shewanella bacterium (found in almost all freshwater sediment) breathes metal instead of oxygen ✹ Oil-eating bacteria can clean up oil spills ✹ Ground and cooked shark livers have been used to create an antibiotic called squalamine ✹ Kissing (often called "swapping spit" boosts the immune system by helping the body beef up its defenses against germs ✹ A "super pox" is a genetically engineered virus designed to overcome the existing vaccine against it ✹ Unborn babies stock up on disease-preventing cells piped from the mother through the umbilical cord ✹ A bacterium can develop resistance to an antibiotic in mere minutes ✹ Dengue fever is nicknamed "breakbone fever" and "devil's crunch" because of the awful pain the disease causes ✹ A 1900 bubonic plague epidemic in San Francisco was caused by infected stowaways aboard a ship ✹ After the 1906 San Francisco earthquake, the rat population exploded and created a second bubonic plague epidemic ✹ The term "airport malaria" or "baggage malaria" is from infected mosquitoes travelling in the cargo holds and wheel wells of jets from tropical countries to temperate climates

©Carole Marsh / Carole Marsh's Curriculum Lab

Surprising Germ Trivia! (continued)

✸ West Nile virus may have come from an infected farm goose, which had been infected by a stork ✸ Measles is believed to have originated from distemper, a disease of dogs, and rinderpest, a disease of cattle ✸ The rhinovirus that causes the common cold may have originated from horses ✸ The tuberculosis virus that infects humans may have come from a bovine (pig) strain of the same disease ✸ Psittacosis is a bacterial disease you can get from parrots ✸ Bubonic plague can be carried by the fleas of prairie dogs, squirrels, and rodents ✸ Pet prairie dogs were the likely source of a 2003 epidemic of monkeypox in the midwestern U.S.—the first cases ever seen outside of Africa ✸ Leptospirosis can be gotten from the urine of infected animals ✸ Tularemia is a disease gotten from infected rabbits, cats, and voles ✸ More than 3,000 people were infected with Norwalk virus after an infected baker mixed frosting using his bare hands and arms ✸ It is estimated that a single teaspoon of soil may contain thousands of different species of germs ✸ Unknown at the time, "natural" cures were actually antibacterial toxins; examples=spoiled soybean curd; rotted roasted green corn, and molded bread to dress wounds ✸ Staphylococcus aureus lives harmlessly on the skin of the nostrils, armpits, or groin of 20-25% of humans ✸ Puerperal fever once killed women after giving birth; it was discovered after the doctor had failed to wash his hands after performing autopsies ✸ Germs hiding beneath the extremely long fingernails of nurses killed 16 newborn babies in an Oklahoma City hospital ✸ Leishmania braziliensis is a microscopic protozoan that can rot away the lower half of the face and leave you unable to speak ✸ To research blood-borne infections, scientists take samples from the penises of mummies because that is where ancient blood is more apt to survive intact

Sources: HOT ZONES for KIDS by Carole Marsh; 505 Flabbergasting Facts About Germs by Carole Marsh

GLOSSARY
Additional Words & Terms

aerosolized: viral particles that spread through the air and can be inhaled

adjuvants: specially-formulated vaccines with extra ingredients to make them have as strong a response in older people as in younger people

biocontainment: labs designated I, II, III or IV are where dangerous, deadly, highly contagious pathogens are kept; a hazmat suit is a must!

community spread: when a virus can be spread in the air through aerosolization

convalescent plasma: blood product with antibodies from someone who has survived COVID-19

corticosteroids/steroids: used with success to help patients ill with COVID-19

COVAX: a program funded by wealthier nations to provide free vaccines in poorer nations

emergence: the initial appearance of a new pathogen

face shield: a see-thru face covering that can be worn over your face, eyes, and mask

FDA: U.S. Food and Drug Administration; gives final approval of vaccines

goggles: often worn to cover your eyes from infection

humanitarian: someone who helps; a type of aid (money or goods) donated to help others

immunosenescence: when your immune system gets weaker with age

intubation: when a patient has a tube put down their throat to help them breathe

isolation: staying alone in a location so as not to infect others

lockdown: when a prison, nursing home, or other crowded venue, is closed so that no one can enter and bring germs in or leave and take infection out and spread it

NIH: National Institutes of Health, Bethesda, Maryland

N95 masks: a special type of mask made especially for healthcare workers

PPE: (Personal Protection Equipment): masks, face shields, gowns, gloves, and goggles to keep healthcare workers safe

reintroduction: when a virus continues to spread anywhere in the world, there is the risk that it returns and starts the infection cycle all over again

spillover: when an animal germ jumps to infect humans

superspreader; superspreaders: person who sheds a lot of virus and so can spread disease farther and faster; event where people gather in large numbers, contract a disease, then spread it to others

surge: a spike or increase in infections

vaccine hesitancy: fear of getting a vaccine

ventilator: a machine that can breathe for a person

wave: a rise, plateau, then drop in infections

BIBLIOGRAPHY FOR STUDENTS

A Kid's Official Guide to Germs: Our Enemies and Our Friends by Carole Marsh

Microbiology: It's a Small World by Dan Green, Basher Science

GET WELL SOON: History's Worse Plagues and the Heroes Who Fought Them by Jennifer Wright

QUACKERY: A Brief History of the Worst Ways to Cure Everything by Lydia Kang, MD and Nate Pedersen

The Official Guide to Germs by Carole Marsh

505 Flabbergasting Facts About Germs by Carole Marsh

PANDEMIC 1918: Eyewitness Accounts from the Greatest Medical Holocaust in Modern History by Catharine Arnold

Viruses, Plagues, and History: Past, Present, and Future by Michael Oldstone, B.A.

RESOURCES FOR STUDENTS

CDC—Centers for Disease Control website — www.cdc.gov

WHO—World Health Organization — www.who.int

NIH—National Institutes of Health — www.nih.gov

USAMRIID—U.S. Army Medical Research Institute of Infectious Diseases — usamriid.army.mil

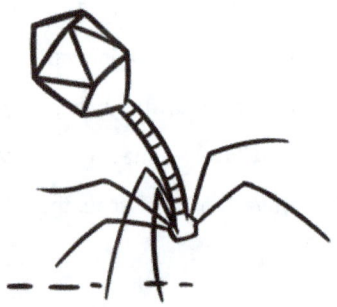

GERMY STUFF TO READ FOR FUN!

Germs, disease, plague, and other gross stuff can make for some good reading. Only you, your parents, your teacher, or a librarian may be able to recommend good icky books to read?

However, here are a few:

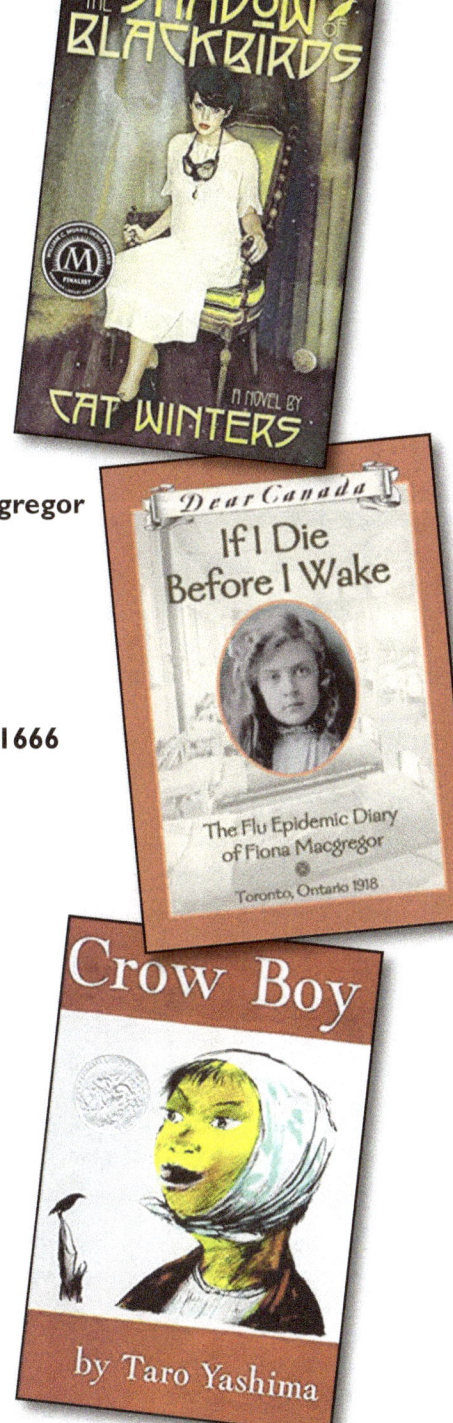

Fever 1793

A Death Struck Year

Deadly

In the Shadow of Blackbirds

The Great Trouble: A Mystery of London, The Blue Death, and A Boy Called Eel

Yesterday's Dead

To Stand on My Own: The Polio Epidemic Diary of Noreen Robertson, Saskatoon, Saskatchewan, 1937

If I Die Before I Wake: The Flu Epidemic Diary of Fiona Macgregor

The Boy Who Saved Cleveland

Path of the Pale Horse

A Sea of Sorrows: The Typus Epidemic of Johanna Leary

The Great Plague: The Diary of Alice Payton, London, 1665-1666

Crow Boy

The Great Influenza

Daisy and the Deadly Flu: A 1918 Influenza Survival Story

Smallpox Strikes!

The Quarantine at Alexander Abraham's

Balto of the Blue Dawn

Fever Season

An American Plague

Station Eleven

The Andromeda Strain

ACKNOWLEDGEMENTS

The author would like to thank Gallopade International, Peachtree City, Georgia, for its work over 40 years in creating educational curricula for grades K-12, its writers, freelancers, editors, artists, and especially Michele Yother, head of New Product Development.

Kudos to Mike Longmeyer, president of Gallopade, who has continued to run the company during the travails of the COVID-19 pandemic, and serve schools, teachers and students in spite of all obstacles.

Any author has their favorite authors and in forty years of germ research and writing, I owe a special debt to Laurie Garrett author of *The Coming Plague* and *Betrayal of Trust*.

To Dr. Anthony Fauci, I appreciate you keeping us all on the straight and narrow of information as it changed so that we felt knowledgeable at all times. The same goes to all the U.S. surgeons general I have followed over the years, especially Vice Admiral Jerome Adams, who drew the COVID card during his tenure!

Many thanks to the CDC, WHO, NIH and others that look after our health all the time. Now we know why you exist. We appreciate your timely and extensive online information and updates. I will never travel again without checking your websites.

I thank my own Beaufort county's mayor, Billy Keyserling, who set such a fine example of how to handle a pandemic, hurricane season, and Black Lives Matter concerns all at the same time and with great aplomb. Beaufort, South Carolina, is better by far for your long years of service.

Thanks to New York Governor, Andrew Cuomo, for saving your city, our city; if you had not, was there ever really any hope for the rest of us?

Much appreciation to all the public health workers; it saddened me to see you under fire; your day-to-day service to keep us healthy is a blessing to all. And endless kudos to all the healthcare workers, first responders, and more—you know who you are! I wish I could say "Go to Disney World free on me!" when this is over, but maybe Disney will take the hint?

Many thanks to all the excellent media out there. *National Geographic* and *Smithsonian* were my constant "go-to" when I had to navigate hi-falutin' medical texts and conflicting, obtuse data; your writers, photographers, and graphic artists amaze me.

There are too many schools and teachers and librarians to thank. You impress me and inform me. I could not do what I do (and never do what YOU do—with thirty kids in a class or at the check-out desk!)—without you! I do hope you love my new CAROLE MARSH'S CURRICULUM LAB style of hand-holding (because I really do wish I was there with you and your students), personal asides via my new Studious Studios videos, and my admittedly quirky style.

To CJ Ellison, thanks for the WOW art! And to John Hanson, as always, for keeping me on the graphic straight and narrow. And to Mark Dean for the *Germwise* logo and all help always, fast and with a smile. And to Tracy Uch for taking on the design and layout of this book and all the extra guides and materials.

To best friends Nancy Waterhouse, Caroline Carpenter (my science teacher guru), and Sharon (Spence) Baker, thank you for listening ad nauseum about this project, for waterfront lunching during the pandemic, and for the food, fun and friendship; sisters, always. And to my sister, Suzy Kelly. As Paul would say, "There are no words!" Thanks for getting me through everything, beloved sis!

To the teachers, parents, and others who chose to use this curriculum as the BIG TEACHABLE MOMENT the pandemic really is, I thank you. My favorite page is the one recommending careers for kids, who because you got them to that page, may be our heroes and helpers in the future. We can hope!

And to the students…if you read half of this, I love you! I knew you could handle the gross stuff, figured you'd endure any necessary boring stuff, and KNOW you will translate it all to your benefit. It was biology and political science and world history that boosted me into writing educational materials for kids. I am a middle-schooler forever, and proud of it—and you!

In this book and all other *GERMWISE* materials, any omissions, obsessions, errors, errata, and erratic actions are my own.—

INDEX

A

aerosolized 55, 63, 81
adjuvants 81
African Americans 45, 53
AIDS/HIV 14, 21, 41, 50, 80
airplanes, air travel 10, 15, 64
America 10, 12, 17, 20, 25, 38, 49, 51-54, 57-58, 62, 64-65
ancient societies 16
animals 13, 21, 28, 33-34
anthrax 21, 33
antibiotics 16, 23, 31-32, 43, 49
antigens 32, 36
antivirals 32
asymptomatic 12, 44, 53
autoimmune 36
avian flu 34

B

bacteria, bacterium 11, 20, 23, 28-32, 36-37, 39, 42
bats 10, 24, 48, 63
biocontainment 81
Black Lives Matter 53, 65
bubonic plague, 18-19, 28

C

California 12, 19, 64
Canada 20
careers 84
cat-scratch disease 33-34
CDC 35, 37, **38**, 40, 52, 63
cells, T-cells, B-cells 31-32, **36**, 39, 42
chickenpox 23
childhood diseases 23
children (colonial era) 26, (vaccine volunteers) 46
China 10, 15, 18, 24, 51, 57, 63-64
cholera 13, **20**
common cold 41-**42**
communicable 29
community spread 81
contagious 10, 14-15, 20-21, 23, 28-29, 38, 51, 55, 81
convalescent plasma 81
COVAX 81
COVID calendar recap 63-65
coronavirus 14-15, 24, 34, 42, 46, 51, 53, 61, 63-64

D

diphtheria 23
disease, diseases 10-12, 14, 16, 18-68
disinformation 52, 64
Disney World 52, 65
DNA 32, 35, 39
dormant 34, 60
double helix 39

E

Ebola 14, **24**, 34, 40, 48-49
economics, economy 48, 51, 58
emergence 17, 81
environment 21, 28-29, 34
epidemic, epidemics 11, 13-14, 16-21, 25-28, 32, 35, 37, 41, 47-49, 52, 54, 61, 63-65
eradicated 18, 22, 35, 37
Europe 19, 22, 64

F

face shield 81
FDA (Food and Drug Administration) 53, 60, 65, 81
flattening the curve 52, 63-64
fleas 19, 28, 33, 34, 48

G

genetic, genetics 32, 35, **39**
germs 12, 14, 17, 24-25, 28-**30**, 31, **33-35**, 38, 47
Great Plague 13, 19

H

hantavirus 33
hazardous materials 38, 80
HAZMAT 17, 38, 66, 80, 81
herd immunity 53-54
Hispanic/Latino 45, 53
HIV/AIDS 14, 21, 41, 50
hot zones 38, 64, 80
Human Genome Project **39**
hydroxychloroquine 44
hygiene 17, 28-29, 35, 40, 54

©Carole Marsh / Carole Marsh's Curriculum Lab

I

ICU (Intensive Care Unit) 12, 52
immune system 21, 24, 28-29, 32, **35-37**, 42, 49, 81
immunization 28-29, 35, 37, 40-41, 56, 60, 70
immunity 11-12, 28-29, 31-32, 34, **37**, 43, 46, 53-54, 57-58, 60
incubation period 55
India 19-20, 22, 62
index case 11, 48, 60
infantile paralysis 41
infection 12, 14-16, 20-22, 24, 26, 29, 33-34, 36, 38, 42, 44-45, 48, 52-53, 57, 63, 65
infectious 18, 22, 28-29, 33, 51-52, 63
inoculate, inoculation 18, 21, 29, 37
intubation 81
iron lung 22, 71
isolation 52, 63, 81
Italy 16, 48, 63

J

jump (animal to human) 13, 33-34, 49

K

kuru **24**

L

leprosy 14, **21**, 43
lice 28, 33
lockdown 65, 81
Lyme disease 34
lymph, lymph nodes, lymph system 36
lymphocytes 36
London 13, 19-20

M

mad cow **24**, 34
malaria 14, **22**, 33-34
masks 25, 35, 49, 51-52, 54, 57, 63-65, 81
measles 13, **23**, 37, 41, 80
MERS 14, **24**
microbe, microbes 11, 17, 20, 29, 31-35, 43, 47, 60, 70, 73, 80
microorganisms 30
microscope 30-31, 35, 37, 49
mosquitoes 22, 28, 33-34, 80
mummies 18, 22, 80
mumps **23**
mutate 31, 47, 54, 56, 59

N

N95 masks 81
New York, New York City 12, 22, 40, 50, 51, 64, 72, 84
NIH (National Institutes of Health) 81

O

Olympic Games 52
outbreak, outbreaks 9-11, 13-21, 24-25, 27-28, 34-35, 37-38, 40, 47-49, 50, 54, 58, 60, 63-64, 69, 70, 72, 74, 77

P

pandemic, pandemics 11-17, 19-21, 23-25, 27-29, 32, 35, 38, 40, 44, 47, 49, 51-55, 57-60, 62, 63-65, 66-69, 71, 74, 77, 84
pathogen 11, 17, 29, 37-38, 81
penicillin 43, 80
plague, plagues 13, 16, 18-20, 25, 28, 33-34, 69, 80
pneumonic plague 18-19
polio **22**, 32, 40-41, 71, 80
PPE (Personal Protection Equipment) 81
pregnancy 23, 45
protein, proteins 24, 32, 35

Q

quarantine 16, 22, 25, 48, 51-53, 55, 63

R

rabies 33-34
rats 19
reintroduction 81
remdesivir 44
research, researchers 35, 39-40, 59, 63, 70, 80
reservoir **33**
Roosevelt, Franklin D. 22

S

SARS 14, **24**, 51, 63
scarlet fever 23
"shedding" 55
smallpox 13-14, **18**, 32, 40, 71
social distancing 25, 35, 45, 51-54, 63-64
Spanish Flu 14, 24-25, **49,** 80
spillover 17, 34, 81
steroids, corticosteroids 44, 81
superspreader, superspreaders 81
surge 51-52, 57, 63, 81
swine flu 14, 24

T

Thailand 15
therapeutic 44
ticks 28, 33
transmissible, transmission, transmitted 17, 19, 24, 34, 50, 61
tuberculosis, TB 14, **22,** 80
tularemia 33, 80
typhoid **22,** 80
Typhoid Mary 22

U

United States 12, 18-23, 38, 48-49, 50-51
USAMRIID (United States Army Medical Research Institute of Infectious Diseases) 17, 80

V

vaccine, vaccines 11, 18-20, 22-25, 28-29, 32, 35-38, 40, 43, 46, 48, 50, 51, 53, 55, 57-58, 60, 62, 63, 65, 67, 71, 77, 80, 81
vaccine hesitancy 81
vector 11, 48
ventilator 44, 52, 63, 81
virus, viruses 10-11, 13-15, 17-19, 21, 23-24, 28-30, **32**-34, 36-37, 39, 42-44, 48-49, 51-55, 58, 61-62, 63-64, 81

W

Washington (state) 51, 64
wave, waves 19, 47, 49, 53, 55, 57, 63, 81
WHO 15, 35, **40,** 51, 59, 63, 70
whooping cough **23**
World War I 22, 49, 62
World Health Assembly 40
World Health Day 40
World Health Report 40

Y

yellow fever 13, 32, 80

Z

zoonoses, zoonotic 34

©Carole Marsh / Carole Marsh's Curriculum Lab

ABOUT THE AUTHOR

Carole Marsh Longmeyer has been writing fiction, non-fiction, and curricula for children and adults for more than forty years. She grew up in Atlanta, Georgia, has visited perhaps every historical site in all 50 states, done research and writing in many foreign countries, and now resides in both Beaufort, South Carolina, and Asheville, North Carolina. She founded Gallopade Publishing Group in 1979 and Carole Marsh's Curriculum Lab and Studious Studios in 2020. Her right arm and left arm are her children, Michael Longmeyer and Michele Yother. She has six grandchildren. Her rescue pup, Coconut, is her constant companion, and the love of her life is Bob Longmeyer, 1934-2017.

For further information:

www.authorcarolemarshlongmeyer.com

www.gallopade.com

Carole Marsh/Gallopade International Social Studies Curricula

THE GEORGIA EXPERIENCE, SOCIAL STUDIES, GRADES K-8

THE VIRGINIA EXPERIENCE, SOCIAL STUDIES, GRADES K-8

THE LOUISIANA EXPERIENCE, SOCIAL STUDIES, GRADES K-8

THE OHIO EXPERIENCE, SOCIAL STUDIES, GRADES K-8

THE TENNESSEE EXPERIENCE, SOCIAL STUDIES, GRADES K-8

THE PANDEMIC TEAM & CONSULTANTS...

CJ Ellison, Savannah College of Art and Design, CJ Ellison Art, Chicago, Illinois

Tracy Uch, The Art Institute of Atlanta, Ft. Knox, Kentucky

Michele Yother, curriculum consultant, Atlanta, Georgia

Mike Longmeyer, president, Gallopade International, Atlanta, Georgia

Caroline Dame Carpenter, retired science teacher, Valdosta, Georgia

Dr. Alejandro Garcia Salas, Beaufort Memorial Hospital, Beaufort, South Carolina, Lieutenant Commander, U.S. Navy Medical Corps (ret.)

Dr. Jeffrey P. Schyberg, Memorial Health University Medical Center, Savannah, Georgia

And many thanks to Russell Baxley, CEO, Beaufort Memorial Hospital for his leadership and valiant vaccine efforts. Our entire community appreciates you!

www.ingramcontent.com/pod-product-compliance
Lightning Source LLC
Chambersburg PA
CBHW081156290426
44108CB00018B/2573